volume 8

the complete guide to
Godly Play

Jerome W. Berryman

An imaginative method for presenting scripture stories to children

TABLE OF CONTENTS

FOREWORD

This capstone volume of *The Complete Guide to Godly Play* concludes a ten-year publishing project.

The Complete Guide to Godly Play—now in eight volumes—was initiated at Living the Good News (LTGN) in Denver and continues to be published there by what has become Morehouse Education Resources (MER), a division of Church Publishing, Inc. The primary consistency and leadership for the project during this evolution has been Dirk deVries, to whom the author wishes to express his deep and abiding gratitude as our project comes to a close. Dirk was there at the beginning with LTGN and is now Director of Curriculum Development at MER.

I am also grateful to many others, especially Robin Lybeck, who has been with this project since early on, and is now Director of Production for MER. The two consulting editors for this project were first Dina Strong, and now The Reverend Cheryl Minor. Dina was especially instrumental in compiling the wisdom of seasoned Godly Play leaders into what became *The Complete Guide to Godly Play, Volume 5*. Cheryl Minor is Co-rector of All Saints Episcopal Church in Belmont, Massachusetts, is a Godly Play Trainer, and is now running a large empirical study of Godly Play for her Ph. D. thesis, which evaluates Godly Play's contribution to the spiritual well being of children. She is also my Teaching Assistant in the certificate program for the spiritual guidance of children at General Theological Seminary in New York City. Many thanks also to Jim Wahler, the project's current managing editor. Jim has overseen the publication of both *Volumes 6* and *7*, as well as the 2009 expansion/revision of *Teaching Godly Play*. His energy and creativity abound and his editorial acuity, firmness and graceful organizational ability are indispensable.

The project began in 2001, the same year that the beautiful Thea, my wife and co-founder of Godly Play, was diagnosed with cancer, so its conclusion after her death in 2009 is poignant. Still this is also a time of thanksgiving. This gratitude is enriched with memories of our love for each other and for the children we have known.

The search for a method began about 1960 and resulted in the discovery of the Montessori method about 1970. Our family moved to Bergamo, Italy, so I could study Montessori there. (In those days this was the leading research and education center for Montessori, especially for work with the older children.) We returned to the United States in 1972. About thirty years of focused development then took place before this publishing venture even began! The development of Godly Play continued during the project's ten-years (2002-2012) and continues today.

It is ironic that *Volume 8* includes some of the presentations that have been in development the longest. This means that the "new" lessons are not only well-seasoned but were difficult to write. This capstone volume also includes an overview of the curriculum to date and a summary of the foundational literature. These resources may be found in the Appendix to this volume.

Pines Presbyterian Church in Houston was where the first Godly Play room was located. Huge strides were made during the first decade of development, 1974-1984, including naming this approach *Godly Play*. Much of the research on which this approach is based took place at the Institute of Religion in the Texas Medical Center. In those days "The Institute" was a dynamic center for pastoral care and medical ethics, located in the center of the Texas Medical Center in Houston. I also taught about the pastoral care of children and medical ethics, as well as other courses, there as Godly Play was developed.

Our Godly Play research environment at The Institute had video capabilities and a large observation room with one-way glass. Children's spirituality was also studied in the five hospitals of the Texas Medical Center, especially at Texas Children's Hospital and M. D. Anderson. This research room migrated around Houston and then to Denver. Today it is hosted by St. Gabriel's Episcopal Church in Denver, where it is used each Sunday by the children of the parish and continues to be a resource for the Center for the Theology of Childhood nearby.

Most of the lessons in this volume have been in development since the 1970s. They represent content central to the Christian tradition. The most intense period of development for these was from 1984 to 1994 when Thea and I taught the 4th and 5th graders each Sunday and continued our two research classes each week at Christ Church Cathedral in downtown Houston on Saturdays. Godly Play has always been intentionally developed primarily in the context of parish life, as well in hospital and school settings.

It is now time to set aside the complexity and decades of development. Sit back, relax, and dwell in the storytelling of these lessons. Enjoy drawing them into yourself and then inviting God and the children to join you in their telling. May they bless you and make you a blessing.

INTRODUCTION

Welcome to *Volume 8* of *The Complete Guide to Godly Play*. This volume, like the others in the series, attempts to provide the reader what is needed to present these lessons to children (and sometimes adults). The scripts for the lessons are, therefore, combined with some background about Godly Play. Please consult *Volume 1* of *The Complete Guide To Godly Play* (2002) and *Teaching Godly Play* (2009) to learn more about the method and take note of the overviews of the foundational literature and the whole spiral curriculum in the Appendix to learn more about the theory, as well as the theology and history on which the method and curriculum is based.

WHAT IS GODLY PLAY?

Godly Play is an interpretation of Montessori religious education, which means it is more like spiritual guidance than what is typically thought of in the church as children's education. It involves children and adults, as guides, moving together toward fluency in the art of knowing how to use Christian language to nourish their moral and spiritual development.

A good balance of community and independence, as well as limits and openness is involved.

Godly Play assumes that children have some experience of the mystery of God's presence in their lives. It understands that often, in our culture, children lack the language, permission, and understanding to express and enjoy God's creative presence, or to evaluate what adults and other children tell them about their moral and spiritual development.

In Godly Play, children are taught how to *enter into* parables, contemplative silence, sacred stories and the liturgical action of the classical Christian language system to discover more about God, themselves, others, and God's presence in the creation that surrounds and is within us.

In Godly Play, we prepare a special environment for children to work in with adult guides. (*Work* is what we sometimes call serious play.) Two teacher/mentors guide the session, helping the children:
- enter the space and be welcomed
- get ready for the group presentation
- enter into a presentation that is based on a parable, sacred story or liturgical action (Contemplative silence is everywhere in the room, and in the way the lessons are presented.)
- respond to the presentation through group wondering
- respond to the presentation (or other significant spiritual issues) working on their own projects alone or in small groups, either by expressive art or with the lesson materials
- prepare and share a feast
- and say goodbye with formality and care as they leave the space

THE GODLY PLAY SPIRAL CURRICULUM AND CHILD DEVELOPMENT

Godly Play presentations for children (and sometimes adults) are organized as a spiral curriculum— that is, contact with the lessons not only repeats cyclically over time, but is open to more complex, flexible, and abstract reflection, as children and adults develop. (This spiral is described more fully in *Teaching Godly Play (2009),* and its strategy comes from the Montessori tradition of education.)

The core of the Godly Play spiral continues to be presented as children mature. In a developed Godly Play room and program, children can branch out into the Extensions, Enrichments, and Synthesis Lessons when they are ready without losing the coherence of the core, which they will also see in new ways as they move through early, middle, and late childhood.

The "planes of development" concept, as Montessori called her broad view of child development, incorporated her interests in social, educational, and practical classroom insights as well as cognitive development into a symmetrical *rule of thumb* that groups child development roughly into three-year periods: 3-6, 6-9 and 9-12. When this is applied to Godly Play, it means that children from 3-6 years of age are introduced to the Core lessons, the Godly Play process, and organization of the room. For children from 6 to 9, it means that the Core lessons continue, but with Extensions and Enrichment lessons added. From 9-12 years of age the Core, Extensions, and Enrichments continue, and the Synthesis lessons are added.

This developmental approach is also good for thinking about program development. In small churches or new programs in larger churches you might have a single group from 3-12 years. Place an older and then a younger child around the circle so they can help each other. Later you might divide this large group into two and then three developmental groups as the community of children grows. In this way the older children can help the younger ones make good choices by their example and teach their way of thinking by what they say to the younger children as their friends and leaders.

Montessori took a broader view of children's development than someone like Piaget, who focused on their cognitive stages. She was interested in social, emotional, and educational growth as well as the changes in the way children think. A summary of the three general orientations she identified, as they are related to Godly Play, follows:

During early childhood, 3-6 years, the children are mostly interested in how the class works. How do you come into the room? Where do you sit in a circle and how do you listen? How do you find and get the educational materials from the shelf you want to work with? How do you find the art materials you want? How do you put things away? How do you have a feast? How do you leave the room? The primary thing that is learned during this period, however, is to love the materials and to seriously engage in the wondering with the other children about what the presentations mean. When young children learn, mostly by example, how to love the language of the Christian People, then, a good foundation is laid. This love is the basis on which middle- and late-childhood Godly Play is built.

In middle childhood, 6-9 years, the children who are experienced with Godly Play are now free from their previous questions to work smoothly and confidently in the classroom. They know many of the lessons with their senses, even if they cannot yet articulate the language that goes with them. The foundation for later growth has been laid with their *body knowing*. In middle childhood the emphasis is on speaking and reading. The reading, however, may still be at the level of single-word or paragraph-reading, but even good readers are not yet fully at ease with the printed page. This is why for example the parable synthesis lessons ("Parable Syntheses 1," "Parable Synthesis 2," and "Parable Synthesis 3" on pages 132-152 in *Volume 3*) are not presented until late childhood. They require too much reading, which might get in the way of mastery. What is most interesting about middle childhood, however, is that the children's wondering becomes verbally richer.

During late childhood, the mentoring of stories in an authentic way continues to be of the upmost importance. At this stage children need teachers who are very experienced with all of the stories on the shelves and who are ready to challenge the older child's questioning and resistance. It is not possible to predict what direction the children will go in their wondering and work, so a teacher needs to be ready to go just about anywhere with them as well as be ready to say, "I don't know. Let's look that up together." This is difficult for an inexperienced teacher, but it is very important for older children to experience because they have become savvy school-goers. They are anxious to know what "the teacher" wants and what the "correct" answer is. This awareness also makes them devious and aggressively creative. This needs to be supported, but at the same time they want to know if "the teacher" knows his or her stuff so they can relax and rely on them as their guides. The energy required to help a circle of children in late childhood be comfortable with their questions, their bodies, their creativity, their uniqueness, and their awareness of God's mystery in a community is enormous but the experience thrilling if one can match this multi-directional enthusiasm.

In late childhood the ability to be at ease with reading paragraphs and books suggests to children that they might now take books from the lower shelves of the Godly Play environment and look beyond the pictures to the text. Sometimes, however, this is not to their advantage. Some children might curl up with a book and not be as aware of the community of children swirling around them. They might also use their reading as a defense against an emotional involvement with the sacred stories, the parables, the liturgical action materials, or God's presence in the silent spaces between words and the general mindfulness of the room. While an adult guide might want to move children in middle childhood towards reading, in late childhood the mentor might want to move the older children back towards sensorial involvement, as in early childhood, with the materials so they can once again grasp meaning with their hands but at a new level.

The overall goal is for children to enter adolescence with an inner working model of the Christian language system. Progress through the spiral curriculum provides children with the tools for ongoing spiritual development across the life span. This gives them the experience to understand that the Christian language system can have different kinds of meaning and different levels of meaning. This long term approach provides young learners (and adults) with the tools and sense of community to continue their spiritual development as long as they can breathe—and perhaps longer.

WHAT GODLY PLAY IS NOT

One way to understand Godly Play *is to notice what it is not*. It is *not* a complete children's program. Christmas pageants, vacation Bible school, children's choirs, children's and youth groups meeting during the week, parent-child retreats, picnics, service opportunities, and many other components are needed for a full and vibrant children's ministry. All this is important, but what Godly Play contributes to this variety is the heart of the matter—*the art of knowing how to use the language of the Christian people to make meaning about life and death and find direction for daily living*. Children need open and yet deeply respectful experiences with scripture, worship, and contemplative silence to fully enter into the power of the Christian system of language. If we leave out the heart of the matter, we risk trivializing the Christian way of life.

HOW TO DO GODLY PLAY

Godly Play is something you *do*. Further, it is something you do *with* children. When learning how to practice this art, be patient. Your own teaching style, informed by the practice of Godly Play, will emerge. Even if you use another curriculum for church school and in other settings, you can begin to incorporate aspects of Godly Play into your practice. This can begin with elements as simple as the greeting and how you say goodbye.

In good Montessori fashion, careful attention is paid to the environment provided for children. It is an *open* environment in the sense that children can make genuine choices (among constructive alternatives) regarding both the materials they use and the process by which they work toward shared goals. The adult guides set nurturing boundaries for the children by managing relationships, time, and space in a clear and firm way. The environment needs such limits to be a safe place in which a creative encounter with God can flourish within the community of children. The management of relationships, time and space all overlap, but since people are most important in this mix, let's begin with how to manage relationships.

HOW TO MANAGE RELATIONSHIPS

THE TWO TEACHING ROLES: DOOR PERSON AND STORYTELLER

The two guides in the Godly Play room have different but equal roles. The two roles, working together, help foster respect for the children and for the Godly Play space. For example:

- parents and other adults are encouraged to remain at the threshold of the Godly Play space so the room is clearly maintained as a place for children, and
- the two mentors stay at the child's eye level to help neutralize the difference in power that size makes and to foster better communication.

This safe environment gives children an arena that supports them as creators, created in the image of God—like the Creator who made heaven and earth.

When the storyteller presents a lesson, his or her eyes are usually kept focused on the materials of the lesson, not the children. Instead of being encouraged to respond to a teacher, the children are invited, by the storyteller's eyes, to "enter" the story and respond to its deep meaning with God and with each other. Only after the lesson is presented and the wondering begins, is eye contact with the children made, and that is because the community of the circle is beginning to interpret together what they have just experienced.

During a typical session, only two adults will be present in the Godly Play space; the door person and the storyteller. These are their respective tasks:

DOOR PERSON

Check the shelves, especially the supply shelves and art shelves.

Get out the roll book, review notes and get ready to greet the children and parents.

Slow down the children coming into the room. You may need to take and put aside toys, books and other distracting objects. Help them to get ready. Take the roll or have the older children check themselves in.

Close the door when it is time. Be ready to work with latecomers and children who come to you from the circle.

Avoid casual eye contact with the storyteller to help prevent the adults in the room from turning the children into objects, talking down to them, or manipulating them.

When the children choose their work, they may need help setting up artwork and getting materials from the shelves for work on a lesson, either alone or in small groups especially if they are new. Show the children how to do this rather than doing it for them.

Stay in your chair unless children need your help. Do not intrude on the community of children. Stay at the eye level of the children whenever possible, as if there were a glass ceiling in the room at the level of the average child.

Help the children put their work away, and also guide the selected children who are serving the feast.

STORYTELLER

Check the material to be presented that day. Insure that it is complete and ready to be presented.

Get seated on the floor in the circle and prepare to greet the children.

Guide the children to places in the circle where they will best be able to attend to the lesson. Visit quietly until it is time to begin and all are ready.

Present the lesson. Model how to "enter" the material.

Draw the children into the lesson by your introduction. Bring your gaze down to focus on the material when you begin the actual lesson. Look up when the wondering begins.

After the lesson and wondering, go around the circle, dismissing each child to begin his or her work, one at a time. Each child is supported as he or she chooses what to do. Go quickly around the circle the first time, returning to the children who could not decide. Go around the circle again for decisions until only a few are left. These children may be new or for some other reason they are unable to make a choice. Present a lesson to these children.

Remain seated in the circle on the floor (or in a little chair if necessary) unless children need help with the lessons they are working with. You may need to help with art materials. Keep yourself at the children's eye level as you help.

When it is time for the feast, go to the light switch and turn off the lights (unless in a basement without windows) While standing (an exception to the eye level approach) ask the children to put their work away and come back to the circle for the feast. Turn the light back on. Go to the circle to anchor it as the children finish their work and return.

DOOR PERSON

Sit quietly in your chair. Be sure that the trash can has a liner in it.

Greet the parents and begin to call the names of the children who are ready and whose parents are there.

If a child starts for the door without saying goodbye to the storyteller, remind him or her to return to the storyteller to say goodbye.

Remember to give back anything that may have been taken for safekeeping at the beginning of class.

When the children are gone, check and clean the art and supply shelves.

Sit quietly and contemplate the session as a whole.

Evaluate, make notes and discuss the session with your co-teacher.

STORYTELLER

Ask for prayers, but do not pressure. After the feast, show the children how to put their things away in the trash.

Help the children get ready to have their names called for dismissal.

As the children's names are called, they come to you. Hold out your hands. Children can take your hands, give a hug, or keep their distance, as they prefer. Tell them quietly and privately how glad you were to see them, describe the good work they did that day, or if they had a hard time during the session acknowledge that with an understanding smile and warmth. Invite them to come back when they can.

Take time to enjoy saying goodbye, with all the warmth of a blessing for each child.

When all are gone, check the material shelves and clean.

Sit quietly and contemplate the session as a whole.

Evaluate, make notes and discuss the session with your co-teacher.

HOW OTHERS CAN HELP

It is best to involve the whole parish in the spiritual guidance of children. To this end, please be sure to keep the leadership informed about what the children are doing and how the year is progressing. Invite the whole parish to glimpse in various ways such as a newsletter or Web site—what wonderful things the children are saying and doing. Here are some specific things that others can do to help:

- take turns to provide festive and healthy food for the children to share during their feasts
- keep the art and supply shelves replenished with fresh materials
- use their craft and woodworking skills to make and repair Godly Play teaching materials, to build shelves, and in general to care for the environment.

HOW TO RESPOND EFFECTIVELY TO DISRUPTIONS IN THE CIRCLE

We can't cover everything about Godly Play and the support of the community of children in this brief introduction, but there is something that everyone wants to know. How do you deal with disruptions!

First, please model the behavior you expect in the circle. Then, if a disruption occurs, deal with it in such a way that you *show* continuing respect for everyone in the circle—including those having trouble that day. You also want to keep the focus on the lesson and return to it as quickly as possible. As you respond, keep a neutral tone in your voice. The goal is to help the child move toward more appropriate behavior, not punishment. A summary of interventions might include the five steps that follow:

1. When a disruption occurs simply raise your eyes from the material. You look up, but not directly at the child, while saying, "We need to get ready again. Watch. This is how we get ready." Model the way to get ready and return the presentation where you left off.

2. If the interruption continues or increases, address the child directly. "No, that's not fair. Look at all these children who are listening. They are ready. You need to be ready, too. It is not always easy to be a good listener. You need to try. Let's try again. Good. That's the way."

3. If the interruption still continues or increases, ask the child to get up carefully and walk quietly over by the door to sit by the door person. Don't think of this as a punishment or as an exclusion from the story. (What you think to yourself matters, since the children can feel the nonverbal communication.) Besides, some children actually want to sit by the door person on occasion for their own reasons. Continue to keep a neutral tone of voice as you say something like this: "Please go and sit by the door. It will be easier for you to be ready there. You can see and hear just fine. It's okay. The lesson is still for you."

4. Sometimes you will be directly challenged. Suppose you have tried the first three responses and the child says, "No" when asked to sit by the door person. You might, then, say, "May I help you?" If the child is small you can gently pick up the child or walk, holding hands, with the child to the door person. If the child still says "No" it is time for the fifth response.

5. If the child stands firm and defiantly says "No," then it is time to let the conflict drop by its own weight. You say, "Okay. We are going on with the lesson." Turn your attention back to the circle and the lesson. You may have by this time already rewarded the misbehavior by too much attention. Now it is time to see if you can extinguish the misbehavior by ignoring it. The child may still clamor for attention, but the response to the rest of the circle (with the disrupting child listening) is: "Bobbie is having a bad day. That's okay. It happens. We are going on with the lesson."

As you work with disruptions, you are never just talking to the disrupting child. You are always talking to the whole circle. The children are watching carefully to see how you will treat the disrupting child. They want to know if you will still care for the child, but they also want to know if you can manage this. They want to know if you can keep the circle safe.

This is the most important lesson that a mentor can give—how Christian people live with each other—but this is only a summary of how to manage relationships. Please consult *Volume 1* of *The Complete Guide To Godly Play* (2002) and the book *Teaching Godly Play* (2009) for more details.

Usually the way time is managed in the room will provide the structure that is needed for the children to relax and work mindfully and insightfully with each other. Because the structure of time is so important, let's talk about that next.

HOW TO MANAGE TIME

AN IDEAL SESSION

An ideal Godly Play session has four major parts. This structure embodies the way most Christians organize their worship together, although these parts are often called by different names. This structure has been described in various ways as Godly Play has developed, but for now let's see if this four-part structure communicates best what actually happens.

OPENING: ENTERING THE SPACE AND BUILDING THE CIRCLE

The storyteller sits in the circle, waiting for the children to enter. The door person sits by the door and helps children and parents separate outside the room and encourages the children to "slow down," mentally and physically, as they cross the threshold.

The storyteller helps the children sit in an appropriate place in the circle, where they will have the best chance to be successful. Each child is greeted warmly by name. The storyteller models calm and kindness, attunement and wonder, as well as the joy and respect. This shows how the time will be spent and what it feels like.

HEARING THE WORD OF GOD: PRESENTATION AND RESPONSE

The session begins when the storyteller invites a child to move the "golden arrow" to the next block on the wall hanging that represents the circle of the church year. Each block represents a Sunday and this way of telling time helps the children understand where they are in the church year and in the sequence of lessons to be presented.

The storyteller then presents the day's lesson. When the presentation is ended, the storyteller invites the children to wonder together about the lesson. When the wondering begins to lose its energy, the storyteller puts the lesson away and then goes around the circle to invite each child to choose work for the day. If necessary, the door person helps children get out their work—either storytelling materials or art supplies. The children that are not yet ready to be self-directed can remain in the circle with the storyteller for another lesson.

SHARING THE FEAST: PREPARING THE FEAST AND SHARING IT IN HOLY LEISURE

The door person helps three children set out the napkins, food, and drink for the feast—such as juice, fruit or cookies. The storyteller then moves around the circle, mostly with his or her eyes, to invite the children take turns saying prayers, whether silently or aloud, until the last prayer is said by the storyteller. The children and storyteller, then, share the feast, and clean things up, each child putting his or her trash, such as napkins and empty cups, in the wastebasket.

DISMISSAL: SAYING GOODBYE AND LEAVING THE SPACE

After all is put away the children visit quietly with each other and the storyteller in the circle, as they get ready to say goodbye. The door person whispers each child's name as parents appear at the door. The child gets up and goes to the middle of the circle and turns toward the storyteller to say goodbye. The storyteller's hands are extended, letting the child make the decision to hug, hold hands, or not touch at all. The storyteller says goodbye and very quietly tells each child what a pleasure it was to have him or her as part of the community on that day.

In an optimum setting, the opening, presentation of the lesson and wondering aloud together about the lesson might take about half an hour. The children's response to the lesson through art, retelling and other work might take about an hour. The preparation for the feast, the feast, and saying goodbye might take another half an hour. Few have the leisure of a two-hour class period, as Thea and I did in our research classes. What can you do if your class time is less?

WHAT IF YOU ONLY HAVE THE FAMOUS FORTY-FIVE MINUTE CHRISTIAN EDUCATION "HOUR"?

You may have only a short time for your Godly Play sessions. There are several options.

FOCUS ON THE FEAST

Sometimes children take especially long to get ready. If you need a full fifteen minutes to build the circle, you can move directly to the feast, leaving time for a leisurely goodbye. This will not short-change the children. The quality of time and relationships experienced within the space is one of the most important lessons presented in a session of Godly Play.

FOCUS ON THE WORD

Most often, you will have time for a single presentation, including time for the children and you to respond to the lesson by wondering together. Finish the feast, put things away, and invite the children to say their formal goodbye. This leaves *no* time for a work response, so every three or four sessions, omit the presentation and focus on the work.

FOCUS ON THE WORK

If you must pass from the presentation directly to the feast, then every three or four sessions, substitute a work session for a presentation. First build the circle, then without making a presentation, help children choose their work for the day. Allow enough time at the end of the session to share the feast and say goodbye.

The managing of relationships and time all take place in a specially prepared environment. This follows the Montessori tradition of education. Maria Montessori conceived of the environment as one of the most important teaching tools at the mentor's disposal. A few words about how to use the environment for teaching will round out this introduction to Godly Play.

HOW TO MANAGE SPACE
GETTING STARTED

When beginning Godly Play, focus first on the relationships and how to manage time. While you do this begin to create an optimum environment. Godly Play is worth beginning with the simplest of resources. You can begin without any materials except for the two mentors who greet the children, present a lesson—storytelling is part of many different curricula—wonder, share a feast, and tell the children goodbye with respect and caring.

Over time, however, the room needs to take on the structure of the Christian language system. A focal shelf needs to come first. A shelf for sacred stories, one for liturgical action lessons, and one for parables come next.

The goal for the environment is that it will take on, visually and silently, the whole language system of the Christian Tradition including sacred stories, parables, liturgical action, and our tradition's respect for contemplative silence. The core parts of the language system are kept on the top shelves while extension and enrichment lessons (Please see the overview of the curriculum in the Appendix.) are on the lower shelves, beneath the core presentations they are related to. Supplemental materials such as books, maps or other resources appropriate for early, middle and late childhood are on the lowest shelves. Separate shelves hold supplies for art, cleanup and the feast. A shelf for children's work-in-progress is also important and should not be overlooked.

What follows is a basic map of a Godly Play room. Some of the presentations in *Volume 8* will help to fill out the New Testament shelves in your classroom while "Jesus and Jerusalem: Holy Week" should be kept on the Easter Shelf. "Knowing Jesus in a New Way" belongs on the Pentecost shelf. "The Church" needs to be close to the Pentecost shelf, perhaps, between the Pentecost shelf and the shelf for the Communion of Saints included in *Volume 7*. The synthesis lesson for the liturgical action lessons pulls in lessons from all over the room. Each of the lesson scripts includes a drawing to suggest where the lesson might go in the environment.

Another way to look at the environment is to study an overview of the curriculum, which is provided in the Appendix. Each lesson can be located in relation to the genre it presents. As already mentioned above, these genres are *sacred stories*, *parables*, *liturgical action* and *contemplative silence*. The lessons are also divided into the kinds of lessons: Core, Extension, Enrichment, or Synthesis lessons.

The environment, however, is not just the place or things within the place. It includes the adult guides and their respect for children's self-direction, the community of children as a healthy system, and how all in the room are at play with God. In other words, *the voice* of the mentors and their feelings are also an important part of the environment.

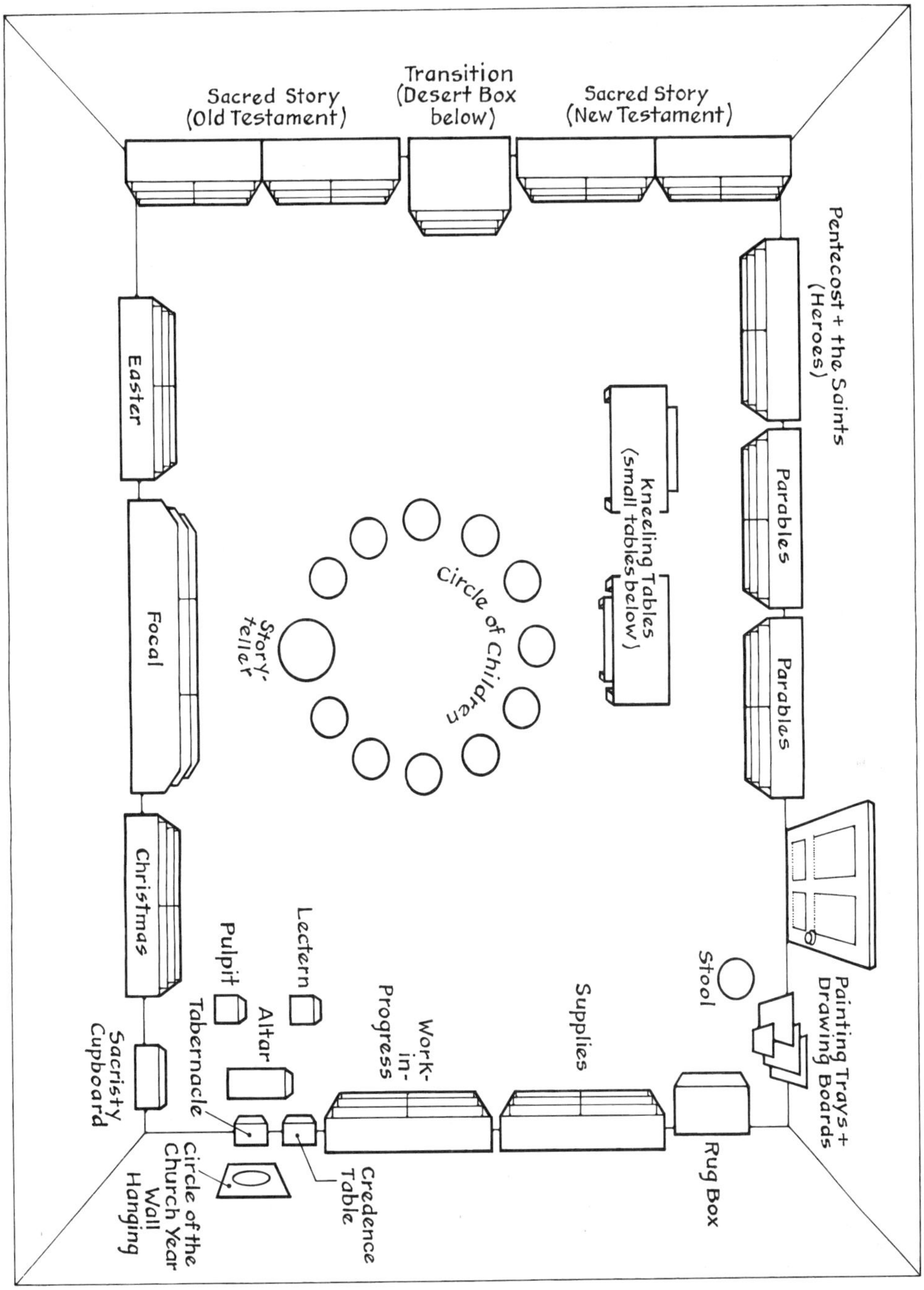
Sacred Story
(Old Testament)
Transition
(Desert Box
below)
Sacred Story
(New Testament)
Pentecost + the Saints
(Heroes)
Parables
Parables
Kneeling Tables
(small tables below)
Circle of Children
Story-
teller
Easter
Focal
Christmas
Lectern
Pulpit
Altar
Tabernacle
Sacristy
Cupboard
Circle of the
Church Year
Wall
Hanging
Credence
Table
Work-
in-
Progress
Supplies
Stool
Painting Trays +
Drawing Boards
Rug Box

THE GODLY PLAY ROOM

USING THE ENVIRONMENT TO SHOW RESPECT FOR CHILDREN
A GODLY PLAY ENVIRONMENT IS STRUCTURED TO SUPPORT CHILDREN'S WORK IN FOUR WAYS:

1. The teaching materials are inviting and available, because the room is open, clean and well-organized. The room needs to say to the children, "This place is for you. You can touch things here and work with what feels right to you, when you have had the lessons." The mentors also suggest that if you haven't had a lesson you are interested in, ask one of the other children or the storyteller to show it to you. Children walking into a Godly Play room take delight at all the fascinating materials calling out to them, but it should also be kept in mind that children with any degree or kind of sensory processing disorder (SPD) might find the environment overwhelming. Mentors need to be alert to help these children relax and enjoy the rich environment.

2. The environment is taken care of by the children themselves. When something spills, the adults could quickly wipe it up, but the goal is not keeping the room clean. It is to help children learn how to take care of their own spills, and the room in general. In this way we communicate to them the respect we have for their own problem-solving capabilities and self-direction. These abilities, as well as their involvement in the community of children, are very much related to their growing spirituality. This is why at the end of work time it is very important that the children learn to put away their materials carefully, to restore the environment and to *locate* what they have been working on in the whole language system of the Christian people. This is why children can also choose as their work during the response time such activities as dusting, watering plants, repairing materials and other activities that care for the environment.

3. The Godly Play room is a place where children's work is respected for itself. The goal is not to impress the parents with the creativity of the adults in the room, or their ability to fashion canned art responses. The goal is for the children to express and work with their insights into life and death by means of the Christian language system. Unfinished work is, therefore, kept safely on a shelf until the children are finished, which may take some time when they are really involved. One project, as an example from Thea's and my Godly Play room, involved a small group of children building a model of the church of the future. It took three months to finish. If a child is still working on a project at the end of the work time merely say, "This project will be here for you next week. You can take as many weeks as you need to finish it. We never lose children's work in a Godly Play room." Sometimes children want to give a finished piece of work to the room. At other times they want to take either finished or unfinished work home. These choices are theirs to make and ours to respect.

4. The environment is a place where a *mindful pace* is enjoyed that allows children to engage deeply in their chosen responses. This is why it is better to do no more than build the circle, share a feast, and lovingly say goodbye when pressed for time than rush through a story and an art response as well. When we tell a story, we want to allow enough time for authentic wondering together or the art of using Christian language to make meaning is lost. When we provide work time, we also want to allow enough time for children to become deeply engaged in their work. In their wondering or their work, children may be dealing with profound issues—issues of life and death. Children need and deserve a nourishing and safe *space* for a web of relationships to develop—God, self, others, and the sacredness of nature which they bring into the room with them—that allows their spirituality to grow from the inside out.

THE MENTOR'S RESPECTFUL LANGUAGE AS PART OF THE ENVIRONMENT

The voices of the mentors are also part of the environment. Here are four suggestions to help stimulate spiritual self-reliance, a sense of community and the humility to be able to listen for God's guidance—not to mention the creativity to bring that guidance to fruition:

1. *Choose "open" responses.* Open responses simply describe what is seen, rather than evaluate the children or their work. Open responses invite children's interaction and respect children's choices to simply keep working in silence, if they so choose. *Examples:*
"Hm. Lots of red."
"This is big work. The paint goes all the way from here to there."
"The clay is so smooth. See how it curves from here to here."

2. *Avoid evaluative responses.* Evaluative responses by the teacher shift the children's focus from their work and the expression of their spirituality to the adult's praise. In a Godly Play room, children are given the freedom to work on what matters to them, rather than for rewards or the praise of the adult.
Examples to avoid:
"I think you are a wonderful painter."
"This is the best picture I have ever seen."
"I'm so pleased with what you did."

3. *Choose empowering response.* Emphasize each child's ability to make choices, solve problems, and articulate needs. In a Godly Play room the mentor's voice can be heard saying, "That's the way. You can do this." Children are invited and encouraged to choose their own work, to carry the teaching materials respectfully, to walk carefully, to put things back when they are finished, and to clean up their work areas when they are done. When children spill, they hear, "That's okay. Don't worry. Do you know where the cleanup supplies are kept?" What children really need is for the guides to simply point to what is needed such as where the supplies are kept or to be shown how to wring out a sponge. When helping, the aim is to restore ownership of the problem or situation to the children as soon as possible and encourage their self-reliance and cooperation to creatively solve problems.

4. *Stay alert to the children's needs during work and cleanup time.* The door person's role is especially important as children get out and put away their work. By staying alert to the children's choices in the circle, the door person can know, for example, when to help a new child learn the routine for using clay, when a child might need help moving the desert box, when someone needs support to put a teaching material away, or to show how to clean up after painting. The guides *show* what to do to solve problems in an unobtrusive way.

The overlapping of relationships, time, and space has now been considered. This brings to a close our brief overview of how to do Godly Play.

SOME USEFUL LISTS FOR VOLUME 8

Each lesson details the materials needed in a section titled "Notes on the Materials." Here is a list of all suggested materials for these enrichment presentations:

- Lessons 1–4: The Greatest Parable
  - 13 triangle plaques
  - triangle shaped gold box with a purple "Jerusalem cross" on the cover

- Lesson 5: Jesus and Jerusalem: The Story of Holy Week
  - wooden tray
  - pieces of the wall around Jerusalem
  - model of the Temple
  - model of the Tomb and Golgotha
  - map outline of the city of Jerusalem on which the wall pieces and models are placed
  - a detailed map of the city of Jerusalem to use as a resource

- Lesson 6: Mary, the Mother of Jesus
  - wooden tray
  - Mary's story icon
  - angel plaque
  - wooden Christ Child in a manger
  - crucifix
  - tomb
  - wooden fire image
  - silk forget-me-not
  - strip of blue felt

- Lesson 7-13: Knowing Jesus in a New Way
  - the six plaques illustrating the resurrection appearances of Jesus
  - the plaque illustrating the gift of the Holy Spirit at Pentecost
  - rack to hold the plaques
  - felt underlay with six white panels and one red panel separated by narrow, gold strips of wood

- Lesson 14: The Church
  - church model
  - small table to represent an altar
  - a low table for displaying the model
  - books about cathedrals and stained glass

- Lesson 15: The Liturgical Synthesis
  - the Circle of the Church Year Wall Calendar material
  - the Circle of the Holy Eucharist Lesson material (Vol. 4)
  - the Baptism Lesson material (Vol. 3)
  - the Holy Family material (Vol. 2)

MATERIALS FOR CHILDREN'S WORK

Gather art supplies that the children can use to make their responses. These materials are kept on the art shelves. We suggest:

- paper
- painting trays
- watercolor
- paints and brushes
- drawing boards
- crayons, pencils and markers
- boards for modeling clay
- clay rolled into small balls in airtight containers

MATERIALS FOR THE FEAST

- napkins
- serving basket
- cups
- tray
- pitcher

MATERIALS FOR CLEANUP

Gather cleaning materials that the children can use to clean up after their work and use to care for their environment. We suggest:

- paper towels
- feather duster
- brush and dustpan
- cleaning cloths
- spray bottles with water
- trash can with liner

DO YOU STILL HAVE QUESTIONS?
HERE'S WHERE TO GO FOR ANSWERS

There are two main places to go for answers about the practice of Godly Play. First, you need to master *Teaching Godly Play* (2009). It is then helpful to review what you have learned there by reading *Volume 1* of *The Complete Guide To Godly Play* (2002). Each volume in *The Complete Guide To Godly Play* is designed to be free-standing, but *Volumes 2, 3 and 4,* suggest presentations for Fall, Winter and Spring and include most of the Core lessons. (There are, however, some very important additional Core lessons here, in *Volume 8*.) *Volume 5* is a rich treasury of experience about teaching Godly Play written mostly by Godly Play trainers. *Volume 6* is mostly extensions to the Core lessons and *Volume 7* is about the Communion of Saints. This volume, as we said, fills in the missing pieces and completes the curriculum. The foundational *Godly Play* (1991) remains a great source of help as well. (More information about the foundational literature can be found in the Appendix to this volume.)

The *Godly Play Foundation* is the nonprofit organization that sponsors ongoing research and training for the practice of Godly Play. It also supports the development of a theology of childhood for adults and related academic matters through the *Center for the Theology of Childhood*. In addition the *Foundation* supports the development of Godly Play around the world. The *Foundation* maintains a schedule of training and speaking events related to Godly Play, and a list of trainers available throughout the U.S. and in other countries to train and support individual Godly Play guides and programs.

Godly Play Resources crafts beautiful and lasting materials especially for use in a Godly Play room. Many of the lessons in this volume reference specific materials available through the address on the following page. Although you can make your own materials, many teachers find their work both simplified and enriched by using *Godly Play Resources* to help supply their classrooms. In many cases, *Godly Play Resources* provides kits for making materials yourself as well as finished products ready for classroom use.

Godly Play Foundation and Godly Play Resources
122 West 8th Street
P.O. Box 563
Ashland, KS 67831
800-445-4390
www.godlyplayfoundation.org
info@godlyplayfoundation.org

Godly Play Training Office
P.O. Box 2881
Portland, OR 97208
503-915 5755
training@godlyplayfoundation.org

LESSON 1

THE GREATEST PARABLE
(THE PRESENTATION WITHOUT WORDS)

LESSON NOTES:

FOCUS: GOD'S ELUSIVE PRESENCE IN THE PUBLIC MINISTRY OF JESUS (THE GOSPELS)

● **CORE PRESENTATION**

THE MATERIAL

● **LOCATION: NEW TESTAMENT SHELF, TOP SHELF**
● **PIECES: THIRTEEN TRIANGLE-SHAPED PLAQUES WITH ILLUSTRATIONS ON ONE SIDE AND COLORS ON THE OTHER, GOLD TRIANGULAR BOX WITH PURPLE "JERUSALEM CROSS" ON THE COVER**
● **UNDERLAY: BORROWED FROM "THE CIRCLE OF THE HOLY EUCHARIST," "THE PARABLE OF THE GOOD SHEPHERD," OR ANOTHER APPROPRIATE LESSON. (SINCE THE WHOLE ROOM EMBODIES THE CHRISTIAN LANGUAGE SYSTEM THAT FLOWS FROM JESUS' LIFE THERE ARE MANY MORE POSSIBILITIES FOR POSSIBLE UNDERLAYS THAN THE TWO MENTIONED ABOVE.)**

This is the first lesson in a series of four lessons called "The Greatest Parable." These four lessons present Jesus' public ministry and the relation of his presence to the whole Christian language system.

This is a *parable*, because Jesus is not a window through which God can be glimpsed passing by. Rather, Jesus is an embodiment of God in the frailty and finitude of a human being. Like a parable, Jesus' life hides as well as reveals. It hides and reveals both the divinity and humanity of Jesus, but also with grace, and to a lesser degree, the divinity and humanity in our lives as well.

This is "The *Greatest* Parable," because Jesus is the source of parables. He is the "Parable Maker" out of whose life comes our sacred stories, liturgy, and contemplative silence, as well as parables. This lesson, therefore, needs to draw to itself and express the whole Christian language system as represented in the Godly Play room.

The goal of this presentation is to allow the inexhaustible meaning and linguistic complexity of Jesus to shine through with a kind of deep simplicity that it is open to people of all ages and stages of faith development.

BACKGROUND

The background to this presentation is our whole history as Christian People. We have followed the elusive presence of God from the creation itself to the journey's culmination in Jesus, and then on to the present. This long story of our origins includes both the stability of this revelation and an open door for the journey to continue—all with the same creativity we began with.

As Samuel Terrien writes in *The Elusive Presence: Toward a New Biblical Theology* (1978): "When presence is 'guaranteed' to human senses or reason, it is no longer real presence. The proprietary sight of the glory destroys the vision, whether in the temple of Zion or in the Eucharistic body. ... In biblical faith, presence eludes but does not delude (476)." Our longing for God is both a yearning for the stability of a rock and the flowing of a living spring in the desert, as the psalms so vividly express. It is the ever-changing reality of a trusted relationship.

The guarantee against turning Jesus into an idol or cliché is that we have four Gospels rather than just one. The creative mix of the first four interpretations of Jesus' life, death, and resurrection continues to generate new meaning and insight about the stable yet elusive presence of our redemptive companion for the journey.

This lesson provides a framework for continued reflection and creative insight about Jesus' elusive presence. Its complexity is focused on a simple framework within which the children (and adults) can deepen their relationship with Jesus in an expanding way, rather than reducing it to something superficial that lacks respect for both children and for Jesus' life, death, and resurrection.

This lesson can stand alone, but it is not intended to just tell the story of Jesus' public ministry. It is also intended *to show*—in the context of a Godly Play room—how Jesus is the source of the Christian language system, which is both our way for making personal, existential meaning and our way for living together in community.

Present this lesson when the curiosity of the children pushes for it or when you, as the storyteller, feel especially called to invite them to become involved in it. Since Jesus comes, called or uncalled, this approach to timing can be disruptive to schedules and long-range plans, which is appropriate.

NOTES ON THE MATERIAL

The thirteen triangle-shaped images fit together in two hexagons to tell the story of Jesus' public ministry. The triangles are arranged in three groups. The first group is gold on the back and shows the beginning, middle, and ending of the story by evoking The Annunciation, The Transfiguration, and The Resurrection. These three events in Jesus' life integrate the stories of his ministry in Galilee and Judea, which form the two hexagons. The gold triangles of the Annunciation and the Resurrection complete the hexagons and The Transfiguration joins them into one story.

The colors on the backs of the triangles are significant. The gold on the first three triangles marks three key moments in Jesus' life when God's presence was especially evident. The blue on the first five triangles signifies one of the traditional colors for Mary and the blue water of the Sea of Galilee for Jesus' Galilean ministry. The gray on the second set of five triangles suggests the walls of Jerusalem and the great stone, which shut Jesus in the tomb that could not hold him.

The gold, triangular box, which contains the thirteen triangles, stands up on its base to suggest its relation to the sacred stories and its key position in the Godly Play room. The gold color and lid to the box link it to the parables. The purple cross on the container's top links the lesson to the Liturgical Action materials, especially "The Faces of Easter," which is presented during the season of Lent. The relation to contemplative silence is evident during the silent part of the presentation, which uses the color side of the thirteen triangles rather than the picture side.

The thirteen story triangles are only a little larger than the fifteen, gold "I-Am" triangles in "Parable Synthesis 2" (*The Complete Guide to Godly Play*, *Volume 4*). This suggests the implicit link between Jesus' self-identity statements and this presentation, which is only one of many other connections to the lessons in the Godly Play room. Everything is connected to everything else, because the room, as a whole, evokes the entire Christian language system that flows out of and returns to Jesus.

This lesson without words helps children visualize the pattern of the triangles and gives emphasis to the concluding gestures. You can do this as the lesson for the day, or when the curiosity of a smaller group gathers them around it during the work period.

STORYTELLING TIP

Before presenting this lesson, please check the material to be sure the triangle plaques are in the proper order so you will not be searching for the right plaque during the presentation.

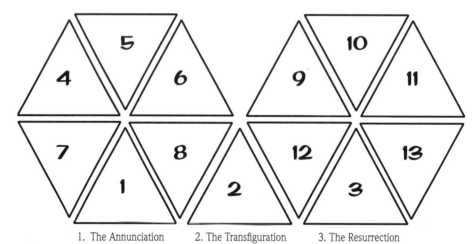

1. The Annunciation
2. The Transfiguration
3. The Resurrection
4. Rejection at Home: Blindness
5. The Twelve Disciples: Calling Followers
6. The Sermon on the Mount: Teaching/Blessing
7. Feeding the 5000: Communion with Followers
8. Walking in the Fields of Grain: Sabbath Rest
9. The Healing of Bartimaeus: Blindness
10. Blessing the Children: Calling Followers
11. The Summary of the Law: Teaching
12. The Meal with Zaccaeus: Communion with Sinners
13. The Anointing of Jesus in Bethany: Sabbath Rest

THE 13 TRIANGULAR IMAGES FOR THE GREATEST PARABLE LESSONS IN THEIR ORDER OF PRESENTATION AND FINAL CONFIGURATION (FROM THE CHILDREN'S PERSPECTIVE)

WHERE TO FIND MATERIALS

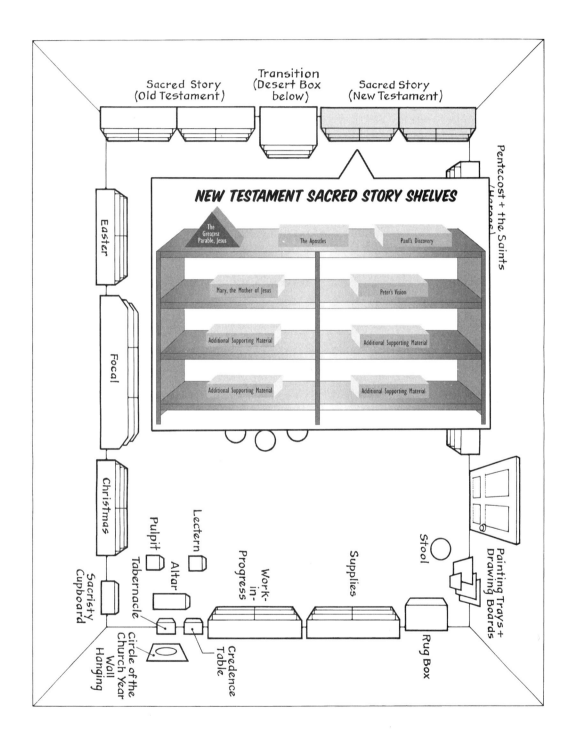

Sacred Story (Old Testament)

Transition (Desert Box below)

Sacred Story (New Testament)

Pentecost + the Saints (Heroes)

NEW TESTAMENT SACRED STORY SHELVES

The Greatest Parable, Jesus

The Apostles

Paul's Discovery

Mary, the Mother of Jesus

Peter's Vision

Additional Supporting Material

Additional Supporting Material

Additional Supporting Material

Additional Supporting Material

Easter

Focal

Christmas

Sacristy Cupboard

Pulpit

Lectern

Altar

Tabernacle

Work-in-Progress

Supplies

Stool

Painting Trays + Drawing Boards

Rug Box

Credence Table

Circle of the Church Year Wall Hanging

MOVEMENTS	**WORDS**
Walk over to the triangular box and stand by it. ➠	Hmm. What do you think about *this* box? It is very curious.

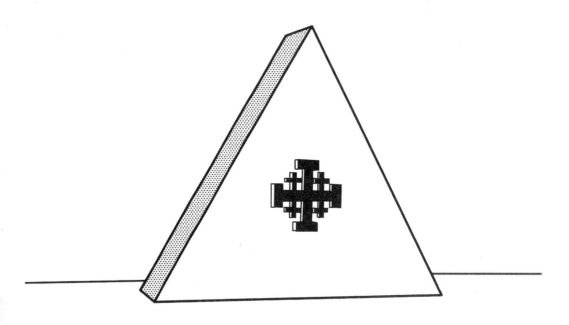

Pick it up and hold it. Turn it around, looking at it from all sides. ➠	What shall we do with it?
Bring "The Greatest Parable" from the New Testament shelves to the circle and place it, standing on its base, in the middle of the circle. Let it stand for a moment and then lay it down flat with the base toward the children. ➠	Shall we open it? You need to be really ready, but I would like to try. One reason this lesson is so strange is that there are no words! This means that you will need to be very, very ready for us to go on. Can you do this?
Wait for the children to get ready. ➠	Okay. Good. I will open the box
Remove the lid and peer into the box. After a moment of curiosity about what might be inside, you place the box in the lid and move the box to your right side.	
Take out the first plaque. Look confused as you try to put it down on the floor.	

MOVEMENTS	WORDS
Look inside the box again to confirm this.	Wait a minute. There is no underlay.
Look around the room.	No. There is no underlay. What are we going to do?
Get up and go to the "Circle of the Holy Eucharist" on the Easter shelf. Bring it to the circle. Place it beside you on your left.	Did you know this box has the whole room inside of it? I know that sounds strange, but if this is true there must be something in the room we can use for an underlay. Let's see. Watch.
Note: *You might get another underlay such as from the "Parable of the Good Shepherd" if you do not have this lesson in your room. If you do not have a Godly Play room to use, then order an underlay from Godly Play Resources.*	
Take out the underlay for the "Circle of the Holy Eucharist." Smooth out the large green circle and then sit for a moment, looking at it. Wait to see if the children notice links to other lessons. There are many. If nothing is suggested, then proceed.	This will make a good enough underlay for today. It may not be quite big enough, but that's okay. This lesson is really bigger than any underlay or anything else. Okay. We have everything we need to begin.
Look into the box again and then back at the children.	Watch carefully. I am going to go very fast. The most important part of this lesson is at the end.
Lay out the first three triangles smoothly and rapidly. Turn them over so the gold backs show when you place them—from your right to your left with the flat base of each plaque toward the children.	
Place the first blue triangle to your right with the base toward the children. To its left place the next blue one with the point toward the children and then to its left, place the third blue triangle with the base facing the children.	

MOVEMENTS	**WORDS**

Next you place the fourth blue triangle below the first one so their bases touch. The fifth blue one is placed below the third so their bases also touch.

You now have a hexagon to your right except for a single triangular space. The first gold triangle will be pushed into that empty space in a moment.

Quickly lay out the five gray triangles to your left of the blue hexagon, following the same pattern as described for the blue triangles.

Turn your attention back to the three gold triangles. Pull them up into the hexagons. You then smoothly push all the triangles together to make one figure.

You now have completed the two hexagons with the gold triangle connecting them, but an empty, triangular space remains in front of you.

Stretch out your arms, like you are taking in the whole room and your community of worship as well as the whole Church extending all the way back to Jesus himself. Sweep your arms around and down to touch the centers of the two hexagons with your hands at the same time.

Look at the children without speaking and make the same gesture again. This time, bring your hands down into the open space near you to show the children how you are inviting them symbolically into the empty space. Place your open hands on the floor in the open space and leave them there for a moment.

MOVEMENTS	WORDS

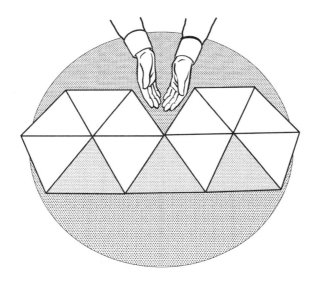

VIEW FROM THE CHILDREN'S PERSPECTIVE

Turn your hands over and lift them up together above your head. Hold them aloft briefly and then slowly bring them down to your sides. Keep your eyes on the material in front of you. Wait a moment before speaking. Smile and look at the children.	There. That was the lesson without words. One day, perhaps, you will want to see the lesson *with* words. Tell me when you are ready and we will do that.
First, put the triangles of Judea away, then Galilee, and then the three gold triangles, so the lesson will be in order for the next time it is presented. Replace the triangles with the pictures face up. Fold up the underlay and place it in its tray beside you.	Now watch while I put everything back into the box.
You then get up without speaking and put the "Circle of the Holy Eucharist" back on the Easter shelf and "The Greatest Parable" back on the New Testament shelf, standing up.	
You then invite the children to get out their work, if this was the lesson for the day.	

LESSON 2

THE GREATEST PARABLE
(THE PRESENTATION WITH WORDS, PART 1)
THREE KEY MOMENTS OF PRESENCE

LESSON NOTES:

FOCUS: GOD'S ELUSIVE PRESENCE IN THE PUBLIC MINISTRY OF JESUS (JOHN 1:1-18, LUKE 1:26-35, MATTHEW 17:1-9, MARK 9:2-8, LUKE 9:28-36, MATTHEW 28:1-10, MARK 16:1-8, LUKE 24:1-11, JOHN 20:1-18)

● **CORE PRESENTATION**

THE MATERIAL

● **LOCATION: NEW TESTAMENT SHELF**

● **PIECES: THIRTEEN TRIANGLE-SHAPED PLAQUES WITH ILLUSTRATIONS ON ONE SIDE AND COLORS ON THE OTHER, GOLD TRIANGULAR BOX WITH PURPLE "JERUSALEM CROSS" ON THE COVER**

● **UNDERLAY: BORROWED FROM "THE CIRCLE OF THE HOLY EUCHARIST," "THE PARABLE OF THE GOOD SHEPHERD," OR ANOTHER APPROPRIATE LESSON. (SINCE THE WHOLE ROOM EMBODIES THE CHRISTIAN LANGUAGE SYSTEM THAT FLOWS FROM JESUS' LIFE THERE ARE MANY MORE POSSIBILITIES FOR POSSIBLE UNDERLAYS THAN THE TWO MENTIONED ABOVE.)**

This is the second lesson in a series of four lessons called "The Greatest Parable." This is the first presentation with words. These four lessons present Jesus' public ministry and the relation of his presence to the whole Christian language system.

This is a *parable*, because Jesus is not a window through which God can be glimpsed passing by. Rather, Jesus is an embodiment of God in the frailty and finitude of a human being. Like a parable, Jesus' life hides as well as reveals. It hides and reveals both the divinity and humanity of Jesus, but also with grace, and to a lesser degree, the divinity and humanity in our lives as well.

This is "The *Greatest* Parable," because Jesus is the source of parables. He is the "Parable Maker" out of whose life comes our sacred stories, liturgy, and contemplative silence, as well as parables. This lesson, therefore, needs to draw to itself and express the whole Christian language system as represented in the Godly Play room.

The goal of this presentation is to allow the inexhaustible meaning and linguistic complexity of Jesus to shine through with a kind of deep simplicity that it is open to people of all ages and stages of faith development.

BACKGROUND

The background to this presentation is our whole history as Christian People. We have followed the elusive presence of God from the creation itself to the journey's culmination in Jesus, and then on to the present. This long story of our origins includes both the stability of this revelation and an open door for the journey to continue—all with the same creativity we began with.

As Samuel Terrien writes in *The Elusive Presence: Toward a New Biblical Theology* (1978): "When presence is 'guaranteed' to human senses or reason, it is no longer real presence. The proprietary sight of the glory destroys the vision, whether in the temple of Zion or in the Eucharistic body. … In biblical faith, presence eludes but does not delude (476)." Our longing for God is both a yearning for the stability of a rock and the flowing of a living spring in the desert, as the psalms so vividly express. It is the ever-changing reality of a trusted relationship.

The guarantee against turning Jesus into an idol or cliché is that we have four Gospels rather than just one. The creative mix of the first four interpretations of Jesus' life, death, and resurrection continues to generate new meaning and insight about the stable yet elusive presence of our redemptive companion for the journey.

This lesson provides a framework for continued reflection and creative insight about Jesus' elusive presence. Its complexity is focused on a simple framework within which the children (and adults) can deepen their relationship with Jesus in an expanding way, rather than reducing it to something superficial that lacks respect for both children and for Jesus' life, death, and resurrection.

This lesson can stand alone, but it is not intended to just tell the story of Jesus' public ministry. It is also intended *to show*—in the context of a Godly Play room—how Jesus is the source of the Christian language system, which is both our way for making personal, existential meaning and our way for living together in community.

Present this lesson when the curiosity of the children pushes for it or when you, as the storyteller, feel especially called to invite them to become involved in it. Since Jesus comes, called or uncalled, this approach to timing can be disruptive to schedules and long-range plans, which is appropriate.

NOTES ON THE MATERIAL

The thirteen triangle-shaped images fit together in two hexagons to tell the story of Jesus' public ministry. The triangles are arranged in three groups. The first group is gold on the back and shows the beginning, middle, and ending of the story by evoking The Annunciation, The Transfiguration, and The Resurrection. These three events in Jesus' life integrate the stories of his ministry in Galilee and Judea, which form the two hexagons. The gold triangles of the Annunciation and the Resurrection complete the hexagons and The Transfiguration joins them into one story.

The colors on the backs of the triangles are significant. The gold on the first three triangles marks three key moments in Jesus' life when God's presence was especially evident. The blue on the first

five triangles signifies one of the traditional colors for Mary and the blue water of the Sea of Galilee for Jesus' Galilean ministry. The gray on the second set of five triangles suggests the walls of Jerusalem and the great stone, which shut Jesus in the tomb that could not hold him.

The gold, triangular box, which contains the thirteen triangles, stands up on its base to suggest its relation to the sacred stories and its key position in the Godly Play room. The gold color and lid to the box link it to the parables. The purple cross on the container's top links the lesson to the Liturgical Action materials, especially "The Faces of Easter," which is presented during the season of Lent. The relation to contemplative silence is evident during the silent part of the presentation, which uses the color side of the thirteen triangles rather than the picture side.

The thirteen story triangles are only a little larger than the fifteen, gold "I-Am" triangles in "Parable Synthesis 2" (*The Complete Guide to Godly Play, Volume 4*). This suggests the implicit link between Jesus' self-identity statements and this presentation, which is only one of many other connections to the lessons in the Godly Play room. Everything is connected to everything else, because the room, as a whole, evokes the entire Christian language system that flows out of and returns to Jesus.

STORYTELLING TIP

Before presenting this lesson, please check the material to be sure the triangle plaques are in the proper order so you will not be searching for the right plaque during the presentation.

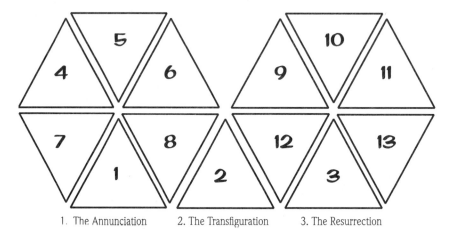

1. The Annunciation   2. The Transfiguration   3. The Resurrection

4. Rejection at Home: Blindness
5. The Twelve Disciples: Calling Followers
6. The Sermon on the Mount: Teaching/Blessing
7. Feeding the 5000: Communion with Followers
8. Walking in the Fields of Grain: Sabbath Rest

9. The Healing of Bartimaeus: Blindness
10. Blessing the Children: Calling Followers
11. The Summary of the Law: Teaching
12. The Meal with Zaccaeus: Communion with Sinners
13. The Anointing of Jesus in Bethany: Sabbath Rest

THE 13 TRIANGULAR IMAGES FOR THE GREATEST PARABLE LESSONS IN THEIR ORDER OF PRESENTATION AND FINAL CONFIGURATION (FROM THE CHILDREN'S PERSPECTIVE)

WHERE TO FIND MATERIALS

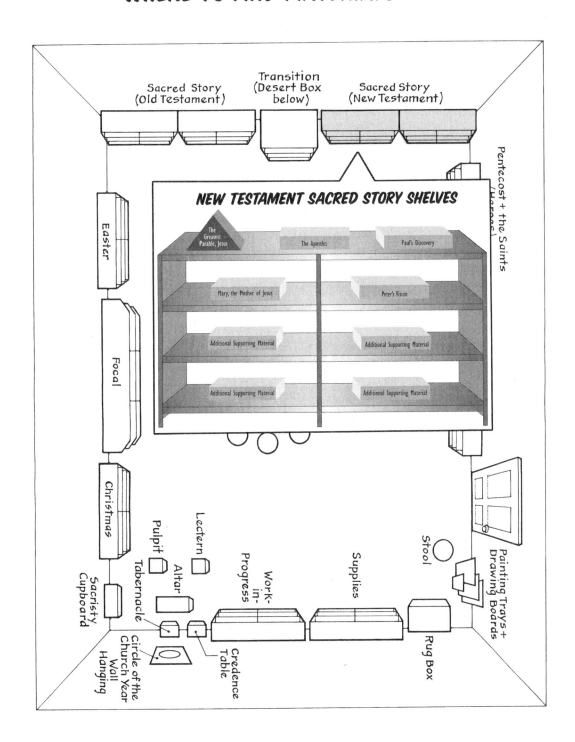

THE PRESENTATION WITH WORDS: PART 1
(THE BEGINNING, MIDDLE, AND ENDING/BEGINNING AGAIN OF THE STORY)

MOVEMENTS	WORDS
Go to the New Testament shelves and pick up "The Greatest Parable."	Now watch where I go, so you will always know where to find this lesson.
Hold up the box and move towards the circle, carrying it with two hands. Sit down and place the box on the floor, standing on its base so the cross is toward the children. Begin to examine the box. Trace its dimensions. Enjoy the weight and shape by picking it up and turning it.	Look. Here is "The Greatest Parable." Would you like to know more about it?
Look along the line of Sacred Story shelves at the variety of the sacred story lessons. Point to them and with a sweep of your hand and a shake of your head, wondering at their kind of communication. Then, lay the box flat on the floor.	This is a very strange box! It came from a sacred story shelf and it stands up like a sacred story, but it is not *exactly* like the other sacred stories.
	Now it looks like a parable, but it is not *exactly* like a parable. It is a gold box like a parable. It has a lid like a parable. There is something wrong with the shape. It is a triangle, not a square.
Pick up the box and trace the Jerusalem cross on the top.	There is something else curious about this box. Look, here on top. There is a purple cross, like we are getting ready to come close to the Mystery of Easter. That's like a liturgical lesson, but it is not *exactly* like a liturgical action lesson either. It does not sit on the Easter Shelf. It sits on the New Testament shelf.

MOVEMENTS	WORDS
Trace the cross again and then each of the four crosses.	Look again at the cross. It is purple, like for Lent, but it also has four little crosses. These are for the Gospel writers: Matthew, Mark, Luke, and John. Their Gospels are where this story comes from.
Shake your head again or make some other sign that you are filled with wonder.	This is truly the most curious box in the whole room!
Sit and look at the box another moment, Then, hold it in your arms, like a baby.	This box is so curious we need to say a prologue before we open it. A "prologue" comes before the story begins, but it is about the story, like the Prologue that comes before John's Gospel. Listen carefully. In this prologue there are many tricks with words. It is about words and *the Word.* See what I mean? That was the first trick. In the beginning was the Word. It was the Word that the words in the Gospels are about.
Look slowly around the room. Take your time. Place the box again in the middle of the circle. Finally, drop your gaze toward the box, which is where you want the children to look. Begin to speak slowly and mindfully to the children and to yourself.	The Word was with God and the Word *was* God. God spoke everything that *is* into being, but God was still hard to find in God's creation.
As you speak about words in what follows, show the words coming out of your mouth and "dispersing" into the room.	Now look at my words, as I say them. Can you see them? No. Are they there? Yes. No one has ever seen God, so the Word was made flesh. God became a person. The Word was born of Mary and sent to dwell among us, full of grace and truth, so we could see how to become children of God by knowing God's child, as one of us. This is the story about what happened next.
Pause. Gather yourself for what comes next.	

MOVEMENTS	WORDS
Sit for another moment. Let the words sink in. Leave your hands on the box, which is still closed.	Are you ready to hear *that* story?
Remove the top from the box and place the box inside its lid. Move the box to your right side. Take out the first triangle (The Annunciation). *Look inside the box, puzzled.* '	What shall we do? There is no underlay.
Put The Annunciation triangle back in the box.	I wonder what we can use? Let's see. I know, let's try this.
Go and get the "Parable of the Pearl." Place it to your left. Take out the large, white underlay and spread it out in the middle of the circle.	This will make a good enough underlay for today. It may not be quite big enough, but that's okay. This lesson is really bigger than *any* underlay or anything else.
Pause. See if there is any reaction from the children. They may suggest other underlays that might work.	
Take out the first triangle. Show the children that it is gold on the back, and then show them the picture. Trace the figures on the picture as you tell the story.	Look. Here is the Mother, Mary. Here is the angel, Gabriel, full of light. He is talking to her. Really *God* is talking to Mary because Gabriel is God's messenger, which is what the word "angel" means. This is called "The Annunciation," because Gabriel is announcing to Mary that God had chosen her to be the Mother of God. When this happened God *overshadowed* Mary and she knew that God was inside of her. In time the baby was born.
Place the triangle on the underlay to your right with the picture towards the children.	
Take out the next triangle (The Transfiguration). Show the children that it is gold on the back, then show the picture while you trace the figures and tell the story.	The baby grew and became the man called Jesus. One day he took three of his disciples up on a mountain. Do you see the three people looking at three people? The three people in the distance, full of light, are Moses, Elijah, and Jesus. Moses and Elijah had lived hundreds of years before Jesus.

MOVEMENTS	WORDS
	The three people watching are Peter, James, and his brother John.
	This is called "The Transfiguration." Jesus was changed but the shape of his body—its figure—looked the same. He was *trans*figured.
	Then a cloud *overshadowed* them and a voice in the cloud said, "This is my beloved Son; listen to him."
	The three disciples were so afraid they fell to the ground, but Jesus came to them and touched each one. "Rise and have no fear."
	When they looked again they saw only Jesus. Moses and Elijah were gone. Jesus led them down the mountain and they turned toward Jerusalem for the last time.
Place The Transfiguration triangle on the underlay to your left of The Annunciation.	
Sit for a moment and then take out the third triangle (The Resurrection). Hold it while you tell about it, touching the various parts of the story, as you speak.	Jesus and the disciples came to Jerusalem. On Good Friday he died on the cross for us and was put in a rock tomb. A great stone shut him in like a locked door. On Holy Saturday the darkness in the closed space *overshadowed* him. On Sunday, the *first* Easter, the women found the stone rolled away. Somehow Jesus was still with them, as he is with us. This is called "The Resurrection."
Place The Resurrection to the left of The Transfiguration triangle. *Sit for a moment and then touch each of the three triangles, as you name them.*	The Annunciation. The Transfiguration. The Resurrection. God came to Mary. God came to the three on the mountain. God came to the women and men who first followed him and God comes to us.

MOVEMENTS	WORDS

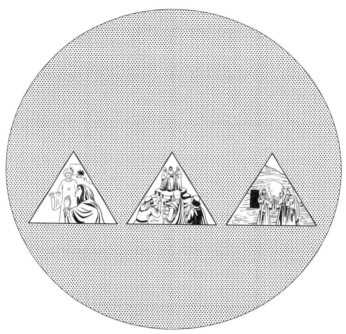

THE FIRST THREE IMAGES (VIEW FROM THE CHILDREN'S PERSPECTIVE)

Sit for a moment and then check the time to see if you can go on with the second part of the spoken lesson. (You may want to wonder with the children about the three gold triangles, but the children will see them many more times and have ample opportunity to wonder about them.)

If there is no time left, you conclude by ➧ Here is The Annunciation, The Transfiguration, and The Resurrec-
placing the triangles, picture side up in tion.
the box.

Fold up the underlay and return it to its ➧ Watch where I go to put these lessons back, so you will always know
place in "The Parable of the Pearl" box. where to find them.
Replace the lids to the two boxes.

You then place the "The Parable of the ➧ Let me know when you would like to do the next part of the lesson.
Pearl" and "The Greatest Parable" back
on the shelves.

Help the circle prepare for response time.

LESSON 3

THE GREATEST PARABLE
(THE PRESENTATION WITH WORDS, PART 2)
THE MINISTRY IN GALILEE

LESSON NOTES:

FOCUS: GOD'S ELUSIVE PRESENCE IN THE PUBLIC MINISTRY OF JESUS (SCRIPTURE REFERENCES FOUND WITHIN THE TEXT OF THE LESSON)

● CORE PRESENTATION

THE MATERIAL

● LOCATION: NEW TESTAMENT SHELF
● PIECES: THIRTEEN TRIANGLE-SHAPED PLAQUES WITH ILLUSTRATIONS ON ONE SIDE AND COLORS ON THE OTHER, GOLD TRIANGULAR BOX WITH PURPLE "JERUSALEM CROSS" ON THE COVER
● UNDERLAY: BORROWED FROM "THE CIRCLE OF THE HOLY EUCHARIST," "THE PARABLE OF THE GOOD SHEPHERD," OR ANOTHER APPROPRIATE LESSON. (SINCE THE WHOLE ROOM EMBODIES THE CHRISTIAN LANGUAGE SYSTEM THAT FLOWS FROM JESUS' LIFE THERE ARE MANY MORE POSSIBILITIES FOR POSSIBLE UNDERLAYS THAN THE TWO MENTIONED ABOVE.)

This is the third lesson in a series of four lessons called "The Greatest Parable" – the second presentation that has words. These four lessons present Jesus' public ministry and the relation of his presence to the whole Christian language system.

This is a *parable*, because Jesus is not a window through which God can be glimpsed passing by. Rather, Jesus is an embodiment of God in the frailty and finitude of a human being. Like a parable, Jesus' life hides as well as reveals. It hides and reveals both the divinity and humanity of Jesus, but also with grace, and to a lesser degree, the divinity and humanity in our lives as well.

This is "The *Greatest* Parable," because Jesus is the source of parables. He is the "Parable Maker" out of whose life comes our sacred stories, liturgy, and contemplative silence, as well as parables. This lesson, therefore, needs to draw to itself and express the whole Christian language system as represented in the Godly Play room.

The goal of this presentation is to allow the inexhaustible meaning and linguistic complexity of Jesus to shine through with a kind of deep simplicity that it is open to people of all ages and stages of faith development.

BACKGROUND

The background to this presentation is our whole history as Christian People. We have followed the elusive presence of God from the creation itself to the journey's culmination in Jesus, and then on to the present. This long story of our origins includes both the stability of this revelation and an open door for the journey to continue—all with the same creativity we began with.

As Samuel Terrien writes in *The Elusive Presence: Toward a New Biblical Theology* (1978): "When presence is 'guaranteed' to human senses or reason, it is no longer real presence. The proprietary sight of the glory destroys the vision, whether in the temple of Zion or in the Eucharistic body. ... In biblical faith, presence eludes but does not delude (476)." Our longing for God is both a yearning for the stability of a rock and the flowing of a living spring in the desert, as the psalms so vividly express. It is the ever-changing reality of a trusted relationship.

The guarantee against turning Jesus into an idol or cliché is that we have four Gospels rather than just one. The creative mix of the first four interpretations of Jesus' life, death, and resurrection continues to generate new meaning and insight about the stable yet elusive presence of our redemptive companion for the journey.

This lesson provides a framework for continued reflection and creative insight about Jesus' elusive presence. Its complexity is focused on a simple framework within which the children (and adults) can deepen their relationship with Jesus in an expanding way, rather than reducing it to something superficial that lacks respect for both children and for Jesus' life, death, and resurrection.

This lesson can stand alone, but it is not intended to just tell the story of Jesus' public ministry. It is also intended *to show*—in the context of a Godly Play room—how Jesus is the source of the Christian language system, which is both our way for making personal, existential meaning and our way for living together in community.

Present this lesson when the curiosity of the children pushes for it or when you, as the storyteller, feel especially called to invite them to become involved in it. Since Jesus comes, called or uncalled, this approach to timing can be disruptive to schedules and long-range plans, which is appropriate.

NOTES ON THE MATERIAL

The thirteen triangle-shaped images fit together in two hexagons to tell the story of Jesus' public ministry. The triangles are arranged in three groups. The first group is gold on the back and shows the beginning, middle, and ending of the story by evoking The Annunciation, The Transfiguration, and The Resurrection. These three events in Jesus' life integrate the stories of his ministry in Galilee and Judea, which form the two hexagons. The gold triangles of the Annunciation and the Resurrection complete the hexagons and The Transfiguration joins them into one story.

The colors on the backs of the triangles are significant. The gold on the first three triangles marks three key moments in Jesus' life when God's presence was especially evident. The blue on the first

five triangles signifies one of the traditional colors for Mary and the blue water of the Sea of Galilee for Jesus' Galilean ministry. The gray on the second set of five triangles suggests the walls of Jerusalem and the great stone, which shut Jesus in the tomb that could not hold him.

The gold, triangular box, which contains the thirteen triangles, stands up on its base to suggest its relation to the sacred stories and its key position in the Godly Play room. The gold color and lid to the box link it to the parables. The purple cross on the container's top links the lesson to the Liturgical Action materials, especially "The Faces of Easter," which is presented during the season of Lent. The relation to contemplative silence is evident during the silent part of the presentation, which uses the color side of the thirteen triangles rather than the picture side.

The thirteen story triangles are only a little larger than the fifteen, gold "I-Am" triangles in "Parable Synthesis 2" (*The Complete Guide to Godly Play, Volume 4*). This suggests the implicit link between Jesus' self-identity statements and this presentation, which is only one of many other connections to the lessons in the Godly Play room. Everything is connected to everything else, because the room, as a whole, evokes the entire Christian language system that flows out of and returns to Jesus.

STORYTELLING TIP

Before presenting this lesson, please check the material to be sure the triangle plaques are in the proper order so you will not be searching for the right plaque during the presentation.

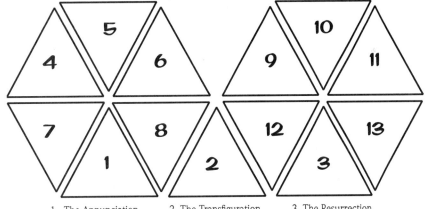

1. The Annunciation   2. The Transfiguration   3. The Resurrection

4. Rejection at Home: Blindness
5. The Twelve Disciples: Calling Followers
6. The Sermon on the Mount: Teaching/Blessing
7. Feeding the 5000: Communion with Followers
8. Walking in the Fields of Grain: Sabbath Rest

9. The Healing of Bartimaeus: Blindness
10. Blessing the Children: Calling Followers
11. The Summary of the Law: Teaching
12. The Meal with Zaccaeus: Communion with Sinners
13. The Anointing of Jesus in Bethany: Sabbath Rest

THE 13 TRIANGULAR IMAGES FOR THE GREATEST PARABLE LESSONS IN THEIR ORDER OF PRESENTATION AND FINAL CONFIGURATION (FROM THE CHILDREN'S PERSPECTIVE)

WHERE TO FIND MATERIALS

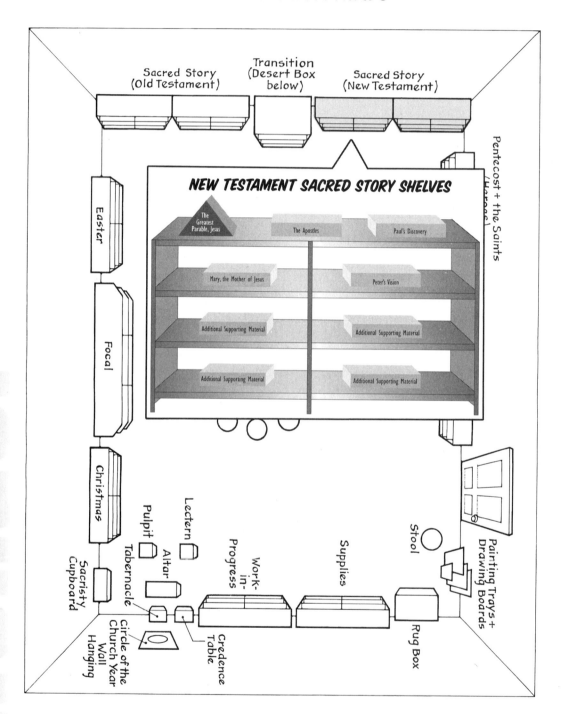

THE PRESENTATION WITH WORDS: PART 2
(THE MINISTRY IN GALILEE)

MOVEMENTS	WORDS
	Watch where I go.
Bring "The Greatest Parable" to the circle. Place it in the center and then move it to your right on the floor beside you.	Here is the box for "The Greatest Parable."
	We need something else, don't we? There is no underlay, so let's try this.
Go to the Parable shelf and get the "The Parable of the Good Shepherd." Bring it to the circle and put it beside you on your left.	
Smooth out the underlay, and then open "The Greatest Parable."	
Place the first three triangles on the green underlay story-side up.	Here is The Annunciation. Here is The Transfiguration. Here is The Resurrection

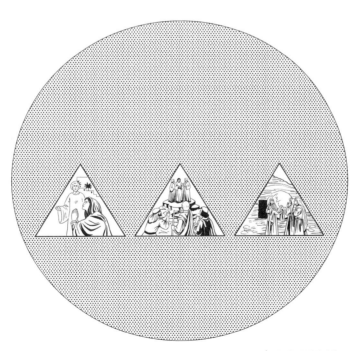

THE FIRST THREE IMAGES (VIEW FROM THE CHILDREN'S PERSPECTIVE)

MOVEMENTS	WORDS

MOVEMENTS

Pick up the first triangle from Jesus' Galilean ministry (Rejection at home: Blindness). Hold it while you are telling the story and trace the figures as they are mentioned.

Begin to build the first hexagon by placing the first Galilee triangle to the right of the image of The Annunciation but closer to you and with the wide base toward the children.

Take out the second Galilee triangle (The Twelve Disciples: Calling Followers) and show it to the children.

WORDS

REJECTION AT HOME: BLINDNESS (LUKE 4:16-30)

When Jesus was about thirty years old. He went into the desert to discover more about who he was and what his work was going to be. When he came back across the Jordan River he went home to the synagogue where he had worshipped all his life.

He read to the congregation from the scroll of Isaiah about the coming of the Messiah. When he finished, he rolled up the scroll and gave it back to the worship leader. "Today this scripture has been fulfilled in your hearing."

The people of Nazareth did not like this. It sounded like Jesus thought *he* was the Messiah, but they knew he was only Mary and Joseph's son, not God's son.

How could they know who he really was? We too might have been blind about who Jesus really was if we had been there.

The people were so upset that they tried to throw him off a cliff, but he walked calmly through the crowd and into the hills.
He thought to himself, "Prophets are honored *everywhere* but at home."

THE TWELVE DISCIPLES: CALLING FOLLOWERS (MATTHEW 4:18-22, MARK 1:16-20, LUKE 5:1-11)

Jesus knew he had so much to do that he needed help. Who would help him?
He began to look for just the right people.

He found his first disciples, as he was walking along the Sea of Galilee.
They were brothers and they were fishermen.

Peter and Andrew were casting a net into the great lake when Jesus walked up and said, "Follow me. I will show you how to fish for people instead of fish."

Jesus then called James and John.
They were in a boat with their father, Zebedee, mending nets.

MOVEMENTS	WORDS

WORDS

When Jesus called to them they climbed out of the boat and followed him with Peter and Andrew and then the others.

Soon Jesus found all twelve of his disciples. They had much to learn, so he began to teach them.

Place the triangle on the underlay just to the left of the first one with the point toward the children.

THE SERMON ON THE MOUNT: TEACHING/BLESSING (MATTHEW 5:1–7:27)

Pick up the next triangle (The Sermon on the Mount: Teaching/Blessing) and hold it so the children can see the picture while you tell this part of the story.

One day Jesus went up on a mountain to teach the disciples, but others saw them on their way and followed.
They also wanted to learn.

First, Jesus blessed the people.
The nine blessings he gave that day are sometimes called "The Beatitudes."
They are ordinary but remarkable things people do that bless everyone.
They hold the secret to being truly happy. The name of the blessings comes from *beatus* in Latin, which means "blessed" or "happy."
The Beatitudes are the true happiness-makers.

Matthew tells us that Jesus then went on to teach many more things, including the Lord's Prayer.
All this teaching is known as "The Sermon on the Mount."

Jesus did not always teach on mountains. He also taught where the ground was flat. Luke tells us about his "Sermon on the Plain."
Sometimes Jesus also taught while he was just walking and talking or in deserted places.

Place the third triangle on the underlay just to the left of the previous one, with the wide base toward the children and pick up the fourth image.

FEEDING THE 5,000: COMMUNION WITH FOLLOWERS (MATTHEW 14:13-21, MARK 6:34-44, LUKE 9:10-17)

Hold the fourth triangle (Feeding the 5000: Communion with Followers) while you tell this part of the story.

Some days went by.
Jesus continued to teach and heal, to bless and pray in the villages of Galilee.
He walked along the shore of the great lake and grew weary.
One day, Jesus and The Twelve went in a boat to a deserted place to rest, but the people saw them.

MOVEMENTS	WORDS

WORDS

When they arrived at their resting place, they found many people already there!

More and more arrived from the surrounding villages.

Still more came. Soon there were so many that some say there were 5,000!

The disciples wanted to send them away, but Jesus said, "Feed them."

The disciples didn't know what to do. They only had five loaves of bread and two fish.

That was not nearly enough for so many.

Jesus told the people to sit down.

He thanked God for the bread and broke it. The disciples passed out the little bits of fish and bread to everyone and all were satisfied.

There was even some left over.

Finally, after feeding everyone with his presence, his words, and the bits of fish and bread, Jesus and the Twelve got into their boat and sailed away.

The disciples must have been shaking their heads in wonder, as the sails filled with wind.

What had happened?

It was unbelievable, but it *did* happen.

It was a miracle!

Place this fourth Galilean triangle with its wide side against the image for Rejection at Home. Pick up the next image.

WALKING IN FIELDS OF GRAIN: SABBATH REST (MATTHEW 12:1-8, LUKE 6:1-5)

Hold the fifth Galilean triangle (Walking in Fields of Grain: Sabbath Rest) while you tell its story.

It was harvest time.

The wheat in the fields was yellow and ripe. It was ready to be cut.

The heads of grain, waved in the wind, full of seeds.

As Jesus and the disciples walked through the wheat, some of the heads of grain were broken off and fell to the ground.

Perhaps, they even put some of the seeds in their mouths.

Wheat seeds are hard but chewy and taste good when eaten out in the field.

MOVEMENTS

WORDS

By this time there were always a few Pharisees following Jesus.
They were curious and wanted to be sure he was following the Torah.
They were careful about this and today was the Sabbath, the day of rest.
They wanted to see if Jesus was keeping the Law of Moses about resting on the Sabbath.

Watch the children carefully to see if they understand what "harvesting" meant for the Pharisees. If they seem uncertain you might say, "See, they were worried he was breaking the law, but Jesus and The Twelve were not really harvesting the grain, were they."

"Aha," they said, when they saw the grain falling to the ground.
He is *harvesting* it. That is *work.*
Work is forbidden on the Sabbath.
They rushed over to yell at him about breaking the law about only resting on the Sabbath.

Jesus listened.
Yes. They might have knocked some of the grain onto the ground.
Yes. They did have a little to eat.
No. They did not break the Sabbath.
They were walking easily and calmly. They were talking and resting, not working.

Jesus then said something like this, "Remember the Sabbath is made for people to rest and come close to God. People are not made for the Sabbath to keep its rules. The law is not God, so worship God, not the law."

Jesus' time in Galilee was coming to an end. He turned and walked with the disciples toward another mountain. What was going to happen now?

Place the fifth Galilean image with its wide side against the image for The Sermon on the Mount.

Now the first hexagon is formed, except where The Annunciation is to be pulled in to complete it at the conclusion of Lesson 4.

MOVEMENTS   **WORDS**

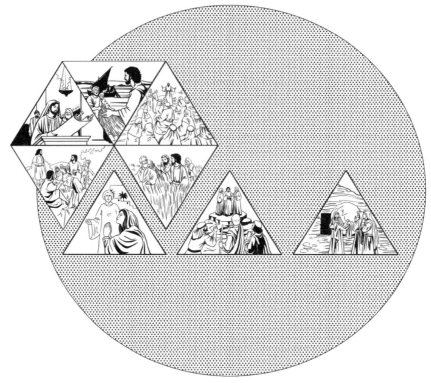

ADDING THE GALILEAN IMAGES (VIEW FROM THE CHILDREN'S PERSPECTIVE)

Sit back and pause. It is time to decide whether to go on with the next part of the lesson. If you don't go on you can begin the wondering. Remember to leave the triangle for The Annunciation still separate from the rest of the hexagon. If you are not going on with the Judean hexagon you can simply finish with wondering.

⟹ Now I wonder what part of this story you like best?

I wonder what part is the most important?

I wonder where you are in the story or what part of the story is about you?

I wonder if there is any part of the story we could leave out and still have all the story we need?

After the wondering put the lesson away, then help the children get ready for the response time if this is where you will end the storytelling for the day.

I wonder (sidebar)

THE GREATEST PARABLE
(THE PRESENTATION WITH WORDS, PART 3)
THE MINISTRY IN JUDEA

LESSON NOTES:

FOCUS: GOD'S ELUSIVE PRESENCE IN THE PUBLIC MINISTRY OF JESUS (SCRIPTURE REFERENCES FOUND WITHIN THE TEXT OF THE LESSON)

● CORE PRESENTATION

THE MATERIAL

● LOCATION: NEW TESTAMENT SHELF
● PIECES: THIRTEEN TRIANGLE-SHAPED PLAQUES WITH ILLUSTRATIONS ON ONE SIDE AND COLORS ON THE OTHER, GOLD TRIANGULAR BOX WITH PURPLE "JERUSALEM CROSS" ON THE COVER
● UNDERLAY: BORROWED FROM "THE CIRCLE OF THE HOLY EUCHARIST," "THE PARABLE OF THE GOOD SHEPHERD," OR ANOTHER APPROPRIATE LESSON. (SINCE THE WHOLE ROOM EMBODIES THE CHRISTIAN LANGUAGE SYSTEM THAT FLOWS FROM JESUS' LIFE THERE ARE MANY MORE POSSIBILITIES FOR POSSIBLE UNDERLAYS THAN THE TWO MENTIONED ABOVE.)

This is the fourth lesson in a series of four lessons called "The Greatest Parable" – the third presentation that has words. These four lessons present Jesus' public ministry and the relation of his presence to the whole Christian language system.

This is a *parable*, because Jesus is not a window through which God can be glimpsed passing by. Rather, Jesus is an embodiment of God in the frailty and finitude of a human being. Like a parable, Jesus' life hides as well as reveals. It hides and reveals both the divinity and humanity of Jesus, but also with grace, and to a lesser degree, the divinity and humanity in our lives as well.

This is "The *Greatest* Parable," because Jesus is the source of parables. He is the "Parable Maker" out of whose life comes our sacred stories, liturgy, and contemplative silence, as well as parables. This lesson, therefore, needs to draw to itself and express the whole Christian language system as represented in the Godly Play room.

The goal of this presentation is to allow the inexhaustible meaning and linguistic complexity of Jesus to shine through with a kind of deep simplicity that it is open to people of all ages and stages of faith development.

BACKGROUND

The background to this presentation is our whole history as Christian People. We have followed the elusive presence of God from the creation itself to the journey's culmination in Jesus, and then on to the present. This long story of our origins includes both the stability of this revelation and an open door for the journey to continue—all with the same creativity we began with.

As Samuel Terrien writes in *The Elusive Presence: Toward a New Biblical Theology* (1978): "When presence is 'guaranteed' to human senses or reason, it is no longer real presence. The proprietary sight of the glory destroys the vision, whether in the temple of Zion or in the Eucharistic body. ... In biblical faith, presence eludes but does not delude (476)." Our longing for God is both a yearning for the stability of a rock and the flowing of a living spring in the desert, as the psalms so vividly express. It is the ever-changing reality of a trusted relationship.

The guarantee against turning Jesus into an idol or cliché is that we have four Gospels rather than just one. The creative mix of the first four interpretations of Jesus' life, death, and resurrection continues to generate new meaning and insight about the stable yet elusive presence of our redemptive companion for the journey.

This lesson provides a framework for continued reflection and creative insight about Jesus' elusive presence. Its complexity is focused on a simple framework within which the children (and adults) can deepen their relationship with Jesus in an expanding way, rather than reducing it to something superficial that lacks respect for both children and for Jesus' life, death, and resurrection.

This lesson can stand alone, but it is not intended to just tell the story of Jesus' public ministry. It is also intended *to show*—in the context of a Godly Play room—how Jesus is the source of the Christian language system, which is both our way for making personal, existential meaning and our way for living together in community.

Present this lesson when the curiosity of the children pushes for it or when you, as the storyteller, feel especially called to invite them to become involved in it. Since Jesus comes, called or uncalled, this approach to timing can be disruptive to schedules and long-range plans, which is appropriate.

NOTES ON THE MATERIAL

The thirteen triangle-shaped images fit together in two hexagons to tell the story of Jesus' public ministry. The triangles are arranged in three groups. The first group is gold on the back and shows the beginning, middle, and ending of the story by evoking The Annunciation, The Transfiguration, and The Resurrection. These three events in Jesus' life integrate the stories of his ministry in Galilee and Judea, which form the two hexagons. The gold triangles of the Annunciation and the Resurrection complete the hexagons and The Transfiguration joins them into one story.

The colors on the backs of the triangles are significant. The gold on the first three triangles marks three key moments in Jesus' life when God's presence was especially evident. The blue on the first

five triangles signifies one of the traditional colors for Mary and the blue water of the Sea of Galilee for Jesus' Galilean ministry. The gray on the second set of five triangles suggests the walls of Jerusalem and the great stone, which shut Jesus in the tomb that could not hold him.

The gold, triangular box, which contains the thirteen triangles, stands up on its base to suggest its relation to the sacred stories and its key position in the Godly Play room. The gold color and lid to the box link it to the parables. The purple cross on the container's top links the lesson to the Liturgical Action materials, especially "The Faces of Easter," which is presented during the season of Lent. The relation to contemplative silence is evident during the silent part of the presentation, which uses the color side of the thirteen triangles rather than the picture side.

The thirteen story triangles are only a little larger than the fifteen, gold "I-Am" triangles in "Parable Synthesis 2" (*The Complete Guide to Godly Play*, Volume 4). This suggests the implicit link between Jesus' self-identity statements and this presentation, which is only one of many other connections to the lessons in the Godly Play room. Everything is connected to everything else, because the room, as a whole, evokes the entire Christian language system that flows out of and returns to Jesus.

STORYTELLING TIP

Before presenting this lesson, please check the material to be sure the triangle plaques are in the proper order so you will not be searching for the right plaque during the presentation.

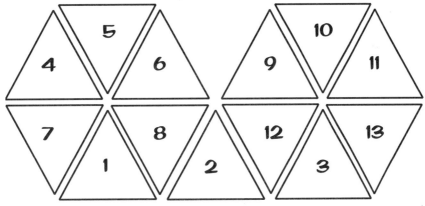

1. The Annunciation   2. The Transfiguration   3. The Resurrection

4. Rejection at Home: Blindness
5. The Twelve Disciples: Calling Followers
6. The Sermon on the Mount: Teaching/Blessing
7. Feeding the 5000: Communion with Followers
8. Walking in the Fields of Grain: Sabbath Rest

9. The Healing of Bartimaeus: Blindness
10. Blessing the Children: Calling Followers
11. The Summary of the Law: Teaching
12. The Meal with Zaccaeus: Communion with Sinners
13. The Anointing of Jesus in Bethany: Sabbath Rest

THE 13 TRIANGULAR IMAGES FOR THE GREATEST PARABLE LESSONS IN THEIR ORDER OF PRESENTATION AND FINAL CONFIGURURATION (FROM THE CHILDREN'S PERSPECTIVE).

WHERE TO FIND MATERIALS

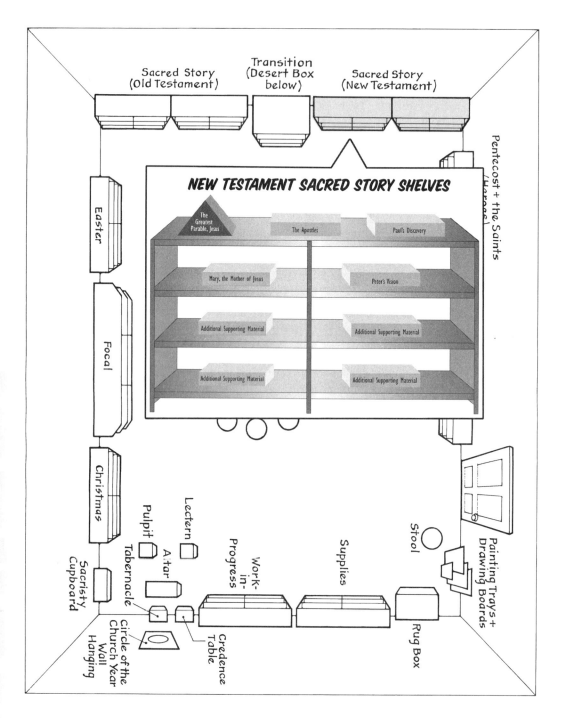

Sacred Story (Old Testament)

Transition (Desert Box below)

Sacred Story (New Testament)

Pentecost + the Saints (boxes)

NEW TESTAMENT SACRED STORY SHELVES

The Greatest Parable, Jesus

The Apostles

Paul's Discovery

Mary, the Mother of Jesus

Peter's Vision

Additional Supporting Material

Additional Supporting Material

Additional Supporting Material

Additional Supporting Material

Easter

Focal

Christmas

Sacristy Cupboard

Pulpit

Lectern

Altar

Tabernacle

Work-in-Progress

Supplies

Stool

Painting Trays + Drawing Boards

circle of the Church Year Wall Hanging

Credence Table

Rug Box

THE PRESENTATION WITH WORDS: PART 3
(THE MINISTRY IN JUDEA)

MOVEMENTS	WORDS

If you are beginning a new story session, begin by going to get the lesson. ⟶ Watch carefully where I go to get this lesson.

Get the "The Greatest Parable" from the New Testament shelf and "The Parable of the Pearl" (or some other appropriate underlay) from the Parable shelf. Place the materials beside you.

Spread out the underlay and place the three gold triangles face up on the underlay. ⟶ Here is The Annunciation, The Transfiguration, and The Resurrection. These moments of God's presence are like the beginning, middle and end of the story, but the story never really ends. In many ways it is still going on today.

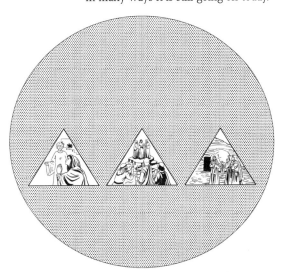

THE FIRST THREE IMAGES (VIEW FROM THE CHILDREN'S PERSPECTIVE)

Touch The Annunciation. ⟶ Here the angel Gabriel announced to Mary that she would be the mother of God.
God *overshadowed* her and the baby was born.

Pick up each of the triangles for the part of the story from Galilee and lay them on the underlay, summarizing each one. ⟶ Here is rejection at home, a kind of blindness.
Here he is the calling the disciples.
Here Jesus is blessing and teaching.
Here is Jesus feeding the 5,000.

MOVEMENTS	WORDS

Here is the teaching about the law and Sabbath rest. All this happened near Jesus' home in the North, where Nazareth and the Sea of Galilee still are today.

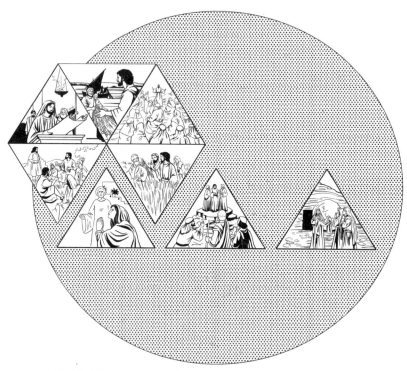

ADDING THE GALILEAN IMAGES (VIEW FROM THE CHILDREN'S PERSPECTIVE)

Touch The Transfiguration.

➡ As his time in Galilee was drawing to a close, Jesus climbed a mountain with three of his disciples.

They saw Moses and Elijah standing with Jesus until a cloud *overshadowed* them.

When the cloud was gone, only Jesus was there.
He led the three disciples down the mountain.

Jesus and The Twelve turned toward Jerusalem for the last time.
Here are some of the things that happened on the way.

THE HEALING OF BARTIMAEUS: BLINDNESS (MARK 10:46-52)

Take out the first Judean triangle (The Healing of Bartimaeus: Blindness). Trace the figures while telling the story to the children.

➡ Jesus and the disciples went south. They probably walked the pilgrim's path, along the Jordan River, then turned west and entered Jericho, one of the oldest cities in the world.
As they went into the city a blind man started shouting from the side of the road, "Jesus, Son of David, have mercy on me!"

MOVEMENTS

WORDS

The blind man was called Bartimaeus. People tried to keep him quiet, but Jesus stopped and said, "Call him."

The disciples did. Bartimaeus sprang up and made his way towards the sound of Jesus' voice.
Jesus asked him, "What do you want?"

"I want to see!"

"Go your way. Your faith has made you well."
Bartimaeus did not go his *own* way but followed Jesus on towards Jerusalem, because now he could truly see.

Place the Bartimaeus triangle on the underlay. Touch it while touching the triangle for Jesus' rejection at home, but don't say anything about the blindness parallels.

BLESSING THE CHILDREN: CALLING FOLLOWERS (MATTHEW 19:13-15, MARK 10:13-16, LUKE 18:15-17)

Pick up the second Judean triangle (Blessing the Children: Calling Followers) and trace the figures as you tell the story.

As Jesus and The Twelve moved on towards Jerusalem, people followed them. Sometimes mothers and fathers brought their children to him to be blessed.
You can see Jesus noticing a mother coming down the road with her children while the disciples are looking at something else.

One time when children were brought to him, the disciples tried to push them away. Perhaps, they didn't want the children to bother Jesus.

Some say that Jesus was "indignant" about this. He was angry. It was not right.
He said to the disciples, "Let the children come to me, and do not hinder them; for to such belongs the kingdom of heaven."
He then laid his hands on the children and blessed them.

Another time he said that if you welcome children you welcome him and the one who sent him.
He meant that welcoming children was a way to know God.

Place the triangle on the underlay, then touch it while touching the one in Galilee when Jesus chose his adult disciples.

I wonder

MOVEMENTS

Pick up the third Judean triangle (The Summary of the Law: Teaching). Show it to the children and tell its story.

Place the triangle on the underlay and touch it while touching the Galilean triangle about Jesus' teaching.

Take out the fourth Judean triangle (The Meal with Zacchaeus: Communion with Sinners). Show it to the children while you tell them the story.

WORDS

THE SUMMARY OF THE LAW: TEACHING
(MATTHEW 22:34-40, MARK 12:28-34, LUKE 10:25-26)

While Jesus and the disciples walked toward Jerusalem, they were followed not only by people who loved them but also by some Pharisees and the Sadducees who did not.
They were worried about what Jesus was saying, so they asked him questions to see if he would say something against the *Torah*, the law of Moses.

They cared a lot about the *Torah*, so they wanted to be sure that Jesus followed its rules and the way of its stories.

One day a lawyer asked Jesus what the greatest commandment was. That was a kind of trick because all the Ten Commandments are important.

Jesus said that the way to think about the Law of Moses is like this: "You shall love the Lord your God with all your heart, and with all your soul, and with all your mind. This is the first commandment. The second is also about love: You shall love your neighbor as yourself."

Jesus said that these two laws contained not only everything written in the Law but also in the prophets.
One of the scribes said that Jesus had answered truly.
The Pharisees and Sadducees went away impressed.

THE MEAL WITH ZACCHAEUS: COMMUNION WITH SINNERS
(LUKE 19:1-10)

When Jesus and the disciples passed through Jericho on the way to Jerusalem they also met Zacchaeus.

Zacchaeus was rich. He was a tax collector, so he took money from his neighbors for the Romans.
People hated him, as they did most tax collectors and everyone else who worked for the Romans.

Zacchaeus had heard that Jesus was coming, but he was not very tall so he climbed a sycamore tree to see Jesus passing by.
Something drew him to Jesus.

MOVEMENTS

Place the triangle on the underlay. Touch it while touching the triangle from the Galilean stories about The Feeding of the 5,000.

Pick up the fifth Judean triangle (The Anointing of Jesus in Bethany: Sabbath Rest). Show it to the children while you tell its story.

WORDS

When Jesus walked by he saw Zacchaeus in the tree, so he called to him, "Come down quickly. I will stay with you today." Zacchaeus climbed down and led the way to his home.

The people watching were confused and upset, because they thought Zacchaeus was a sinner. Why was Jesus going to *his* house?

Zacchaeus did not know why Jesus was coming to his house.
All he knew was that he was grateful and that he saw his life in a new way.
He gave half of his goods to the poor and for every piece of money he had stolen from his neighbors, he gave back four.

Jesus said, "today salvation has come to this house."
They enjoyed being together around the table to share the evening meal, despite what people said.
This was a kind of holy communion.

THE ANOINTING OF JESUS IN BETHANY: SABBATH REST (MATTHEW 26:1-13, MARK 14:3-9, LUKE 8:37-38, JOHN 12:1-8)

The journey to Jerusalem was almost over. Jesus stayed nearby to rest at the house in Bethany of Simon the Leper.
They were having supper.
A woman—no one knew who she was— came in carrying a beautiful alabaster jar of very expensive perfume.
She went right up to Jesus and poured it on his head.

This was like another time when Mary poured ointment on Jesus' feet and dried them with her hair, but that was at Mary and Martha's house in Bethany.
They lived with their brother Lazarus, who was raised from the dead by Jesus.
Martha was making supper when her sister Mary poured the soothing ointment on Jesus' hot and dusty feet.
At Simon's house, the disciples were angry with the unknown woman and her alabaster jar.
"Why waste this? It could have been sold and the money given to the poor."

MOVEMENTS

WORDS

Jesus said something like this to them, "Why do you trouble this woman?
She has done something beautiful.
It is like a blessing.
You will always have the poor with you and you can show kindness to them whenever you wish, but you will not always have me with you.
She has done what she could.
She has anointed me for burial.
When my story is told her story will also be told, for she has done a good thing."
Everyone was silent.
Jesus must have wiped away the oil that had run down over his face.
They finished their meal and the unknown woman went away.

Place the triangle on the underlay. Touch it, while touching the Galilean triangle about Sabbath rest, without comment.

ADDING THE JUDEAN IMAGES (VIEW FROM THE CHILDREN'S PERSPECTIVE)

You then silently pull all three gold triangles up into the hexagons to complete them. Next you push the two hexagons together.

You have now completed the storytelling, but there is still a space above (from the children's perspective) that remains open, next to the storyteller.

MOVEMENTS

WORDS

Look at the opening. Trace it with your finger. Extend your arms to the whole room and then bring your hands down, each one on the center of the two hexagons. This shows how all the language on the shelves in the room are linked to this story. You don't say this. You show it.

You then look at the children in the circle. Make the same gesture to them, pulling them into the story symbolically. You end this gesture with your hands, palms down, in the empty, triangular space.

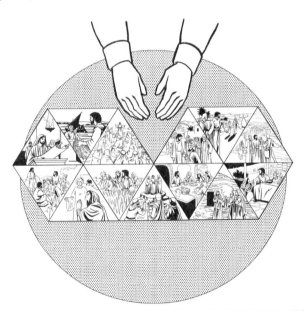

THE COMPLETE LAYOUT FOR THE GREATEST PARABLE-JESUS (VIEW FROM THE CHILDREN'S PERSPECTIVE)

Turn your hands over and lift them up into the air. Hold your open hands in the air for a moment and then slowly bring them down to your sides.

Point to the open space.

Wait a moment for any comments. Stay quiet for a time. The gestures are a good closing for the lesson when it is the lesson for the day.

MOVEMENTS

If the children seem to have an unspoken question that they can't formulate, you might say something like this.

When you are working with a small group there is more flexibility. You might want to wonder with them about the Judean parts of the story and then invite them to make an art response.

Whether you end with the wondering about what goes in the empty, triangular space or with the classical wondering for the sacred stories, you finally pick up everything and put the lessons back on the New Testament and the Parable shelves.

Afterwards, help the children get ready for response time.

WORDS

Now, I wonder what goes here?

LESSON 5

JESUS AND JERUSALEM: THE STORY OF HOLY WEEK

LESSON NOTES

FOCUS: LOCATING HOLY WEEK EVENTS IN JERUSALEM

● ENRICHMENT LESSON

● ENRICHES "FACES OF EASTER," PART 7

THE MATERIAL

● LOCATION: EASTER LITURGICAL SHELF, SECOND SHELF, BESIDE THE MYSTERY OF EASTER

● PIECES: WOODEN TRAY, PIECES OF THE WALL AROUND JERUSALEM, MODEL OF THE TEMPLE, MODEL OF THE TOMB AND GOLGOTHA, A DETAILED MAP OF JERUSALEM TO USE AS A RESOURCE

● UNDERLAY: MAP OUTLINE OF THE CITY OF JERUSALEM

BACKGROUND

Jerusalem is first mentioned in the Bible when Joshua and the Israelites moved into the Land of Canaan (Joshua 10:1-4). They apparently made an unsuccessful attempt to conquer the city. In Judges 19.10 it is called "Jebus (that is, Jerusalem)". The city remained in the hands of the Jebusites until the time of David, who conquered the city about the year 1000 (1 Chronicles 11:4-9). David made this the political and religious capital of the Israelites. It was centrally located between the northern and southern tribes. It was confirmed as the religious center when he brought the Ark of the Covenant into the city. The Temple, however, was built by his son, Solomon. It was completed in 957 BCE and destroyed in 586 BCE by the Babylonians. It was rebuilt from about 520-515 BCE after Cyrus the Great, the Persian King, conquered Babylon and allowed the Jews to return in 538 BCE. Herod the Great (73/74 – 4 BCE) rebuilt and enlarged the Temple as well as the area around it to a complex covering three acres. The Holy of Holies was finished in two years about 19-17 BCE, but the work continued after his death for about 80 years through the time of Jesus. The Temple was destroyed by the Romans in 70 AD and the area was converted into a Temple of Jupiter by the Romans under the Emperor Hadrian. For about two hundred years the city was called *Aelia Capitolina*, the Roman name, during which time Christianity took shape. The Emperor Constantine in the fifth century built Christian churches, and established pilgrimage sites. The Muslims conquered Jerusalem in the seventh century. Crusades by Christians in the early Middle Ages attempted to re-take control of Jerusalem and renew the Temple as a Christian site, but this ultimately failed. Today the city remains a place of pilgrimage and conflict for Jews, Muslims, and Christians.

This lesson is about when Jesus came to Jerusalem for the last time and the story of Holy Week unfolded. This week is liturgically observed in a variety of ways in many Christian churches. Some churches have fourteen Stations of the Cross on the walls, marking for meditation important moments in Jesus' tortured path through the city on the way to his crucifixion. Perhaps as early as the fourteenth century the Franciscans had established a regular route with, perhaps, seven places to stop for meditation. Local Stations of the Cross derived from this. Jerusalem and Jesus' last days are, thus, bound together. Building this model encourages children to re-construct Jerusalem in their imaginations to give a structure and reality to Jesus' last days during Holy Week.

NOTES ON THE MATERIAL

This material rests on the Easter shelves. It sits on the second shelf, below the "Faces of Easter." The underlay is a schematic map of Jerusalem. A wooden tray with a purple interior holds a collection of objects to place on the underlay. They are: Sections of the wall around Jerusalem, the Temple, the Tomb and Golgotha with its three crosses. The underlay map helps the storyteller and children identify where each object is to be placed and to trace Jesus' movements about the city during Holy Week. The story also has a more detailed map of the city to use as a resource.

SPECIAL NOTES

A best time to tell this story is on the Sunday when Holy Week begins, which is Palm Sunday (Passion Sunday), or any time during Holy Week. It is also appropriate anytime during the year when children discover the material and ask for a presentation.

WHERE TO FIND MATERIALS

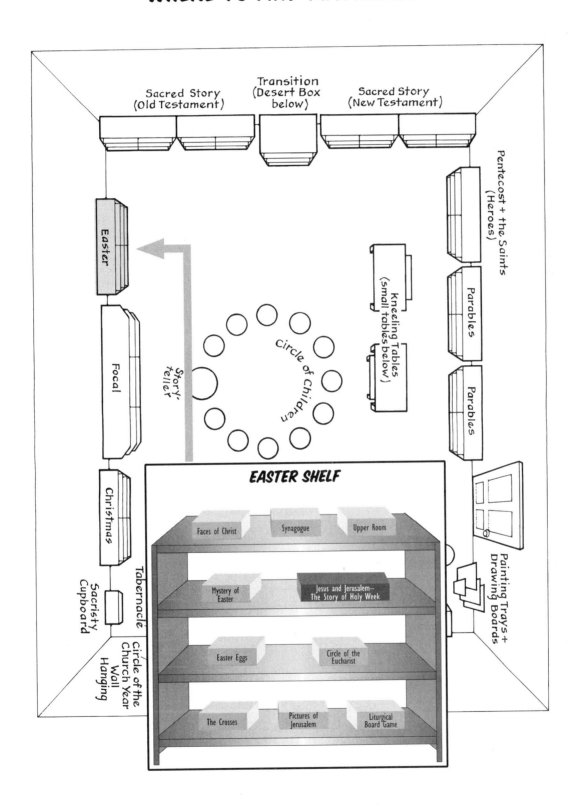

EASTER SHELF

Faces of Christ | Synagogue | Upper Room

Mystery of Easter | Jesus and Jerusalem— The Story of Holy Week

Easter Eggs | Circle of the Eucharist

The Crosses | Pictures of Jerusalem | Liturgical Board Game

MOVEMENTS

Go to the Easter shelf and get the tray holding what is needed for this lesson. Sit down in the circle and place the tray beside you.

Unroll the underlay in front of you so that the southern part of Jerusalem is facing towards the children. The Temple will be on your left and Herod's palace in on your right. Pause for a moment while you and the children get oriented.

WORDS

Watch where I go to get this lesson, so you will always know where to find it when you want to make it your work.

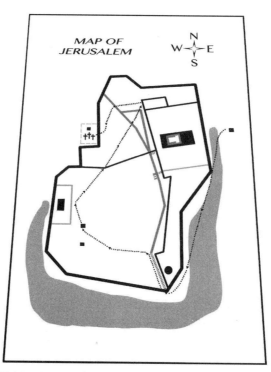

MAP OF JERUSALEM (VIEW FROM THE CHILDREN'S PERSPECTIVE)

Guide the children's attention to the general overview by tracing the walls and touching various places on the map without speaking.

You then begin the story.

Here is a map of Jerusalem in the time of Jesus.
It was already an old city by then.
No one knows when it was first built, but today it is well over 3,000 years old and is a place of pilgrimage for Jews, Christians, and Muslims.

MOVEMENTS	WORDS
Point to the southern part of the city.	About 1,000 years before Jesus was born, King David took the city from the Jebusite people and made it his own. It was there that his son, King Solomon built the first Temple.
Point to the site of the original Temple, which was the same as Herod's Temple.	The Temple was burned by the Babylonians. They took many people, who lived in Jerusalem, into exile. When they returned the Temple was rebuilt. It was rebuilt again and expanded by King Herod by the time Jesus was born.
Take the walls from the tray of objects and place them around the city.	Here are the walls of the city.

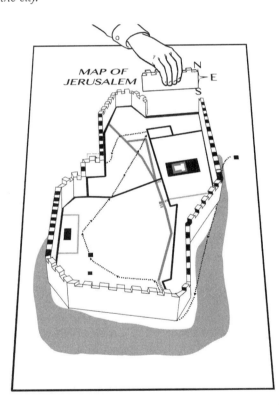

MAP OF JERUSALEM, WITH WALL SECTIONS IN PLACE (VIEW FROM THE CHILDREN'S PERSPECTIVE)

MOVEMENTS	WORDS
Take the model of the Temple from the tray and place it in its place on the map.	Here is the Temple.
Point to the Upper Room symbol on the map.	Here is where the Upper Room was, as much as anyone can tell after so many centuries.
Point to the Roman Fortress of Antonia on the map.	Here is the Roman Fortress of Antonia.
Point to the Palace of the High Priest, Caiaphas on the map.	Here is the Palace of the High Priest, Caiaphas.
Point to Herod's Palace the map.	Here is Herod's Palace.
Trace the Kidron Valley and point to the symbol for the Garden of Gethsemane on the map.	The Kidron Valley ran along the east side of the city. Some say a bridge might have connected the city to the Mount of Olives, but others are not so sure. This is where the Garden of Gethsemane was and still is today.
Take the model for Golgotha and the Tomb from the tray and place it in its place on the map.	Here is Golgotha, the "place of the skull," where Jesus died on the cross for us.
All the places needed for the story are now on the map.	Jesus went to Jerusalem many times, even as a baby and as a boy. Once the Mother Mary and the Father Joseph found him in the Temple area, talking to the priests.
Pause and then begin to tell the story.	
	This story is about the last time Jesus went to Jerusalem. We remember it every year during the time called "Holy Week."
Sweep your hand across the southern part of the map.	Jesus and The Twelve came from Galilee along the twisting Jordan River to Jericho. He healed the blind Bartimaeus and had supper there with Zacchaeus. When they left Jericho, they crossed the low desert and began to climb up towards the city.
	Perhaps, Jesus and the disciples spent the Sabbath at rest in Bethany.

wonder

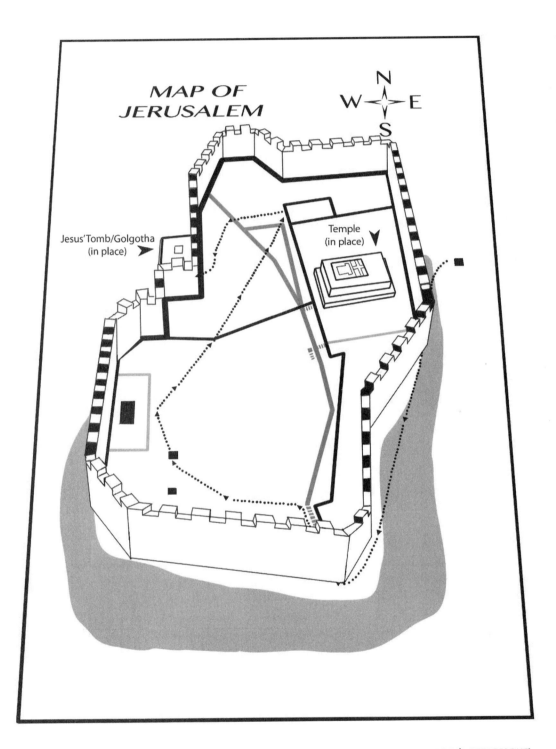

MAP OF
JERUSALEM

N
W — E
S

Jesus'Tomb/Golgotha
(in place) ➤

Temple
(in place) ▼

COMPLETE LAYOUT OF JESUS AND JERUSALEM, THE STORY OF HOLY WEEK (VIEW FROM CHILDREN'S PERSPECTIVE)

MOVEMENTS	WORDS
	On Sunday Jesus sent two of the disciples ahead to borrow a donkey. He rode the donkey into the city, probably through a southern gate and made his way along the pilgrim route through the oldest part of the city up toward the Temple Mount.
Show with your hand where Jesus and the disciples entered the city from the southeast.	Some people noticed this. They thought he might be the Messiah, so they cut palm branches and waved them. They threw their coats on the path and shouted, "Hosanna! Blessed is he who comes in the name of the Lord!"
	Others were opening their shops. Fruit, cheese, wine, and bread were being set out on rough wooden tables to sell.
Move your finger as they walked up to the Temple. Show the two ways they could have climbed up to the Temple area. Move your finger across the Court of the Gentiles and into the Temple.	Jesus and The twelve climbed up the limestone slabs that made a street of steps until they came to an open area. They must have left the donkey there and decided to enter the Temple to pray. Perhaps they went in through the Double Gate. They could also have gone up the outside steps, but they could not go in the Triple Gate, which was just for the priests. When they reached the Temple Mount they came out onto the broad, open courtyard and crossed it to enter the Temple to pray.
Bring them back down the pilgrims' way they entered Jerusalem by, across the Kidron Valley to the Mount of Olives. Follow the dotted lines.	When their prayers were finished, they left the Temple Mount and went outside the city wall, across the Kidron Valley, to the Mount of Olives to spend the night.
Retrace their route as they moved from the Mount of Olives to the Temple Mount.	On Monday morning Jesus probably went again to the Temple Mount and began to teach.
	He no doubt taught where the other rabbis were teaching, along the southwest part of the great courtyard called the Court of the Gentiles.

MOVEMENTS	WORDS
Show the movement back to the Mount of Olives. ⟹	That evening they went back to the Mount of Olives to sleep.

On Tuesday perhaps they came up the stairs inside the Temple Mount and into the long Royal Portico, where the Sanhedrin met at the far end.

The moneychangers and merchants were there.
Jesus became angry about all this buying and selling in such a holy place.
He turned over the tables for money-changing and upset those selling birds in little cages and other animals for sacrifices. He called for the people to keep the Temple a place of prayer.
The guards began to watch him carefully. They also noticed how the crowds listening to him were growing.

Jesus and the Twelve returned that evening to the Mount of Olives, perhaps even to Bethany, to sleep.
The people watched them cross the Kidron Valley again and began to talk about the legend that the Mount of Olives was where the Messiah was to come down from heaven and lead an army of angels to drive away the Roman soldiers.

On Wednesday the crowds listening to him grew larger and the guards became worried.
They began to think about how to arrest him. That evening Jesus and The Twelve crossed over to the Mount of Olives, once more.

Perhaps, as the sun set, Jesus sat on the hillside across from the Temple with Peter, Andrew, James and John.
They asked him privately what was going to happen.

On Thursday the guards were ready to take Jesus, but he did not appear on the Temple Mount.
The Disciples asked Jesus where they would keep the Passover.
He told them to go into the city and look for a man carrying a water jar.
He would show them.

| *Show how they all go into the city for the Last Supper. Follow the dotted lines.* ⟹ | When evening came they crossed the Kidron Valley and went into the city to the appointed house. |

MOVEMENTS	WORDS
	They climbed up the stairs to an upper room and had their last supper together.
	After they had everything they wanted to eat Jesus shared the bread and the wine with them and said that he would always be with them, especially in the bread and wine. They did not understand what he meant, but they would not forget. He also told them to love one another and he showed how to care for each other by washing their feet.
Show Judas hurrying away into the city. Motion with your hand to show him disappearing into the streets.	After that Judas hurried away into the darkness of the city.
Move your hand generally to show the return to the Mount of Olives and point with your finger to The Garden of Gethsemane, as you tell about his prayers.	The rest went back to the Mount of Olives. Now it was late. You could barely see the lights of Jerusalem across the way. Jesus went to the Garden of Gethsemane to pray while the disciples fell asleep.
	When Jesus came back from his prayers the soldiers from the Temple came out of the darkness and took him away. Judas was with them and showed Jesus to them.
Point to the house of Caiaphas.	They took him back into the city and finally to the house of Caiaphas the High Priest.
	There the priests asked him questions, but he did not answer. Finally the high priest tore his robes, and cried out, "Blasphemy." They convicted Jesus of the crime of pretending to be God.
Point to the Fortress of Antonia.	After that the temple guards probably took Jesus to a jail in the Roman Fortress of Antonia.
Leave your finger resting on the Fortress of Antonia.	On Friday morning Jesus was brought to Pilate, the Roman Governor. Pilate asked Jesus questions. "Are you the King of the Jews?" Jesus replied "You have said so," but had nothing else to say.
Point to Herod's palace...	When Jesus would not answer, Pilate sent him to Herod, a son of Herod the Great, who built the Temple and had died about thirty-four years before.

MOVEMENTS	WORDS
... and then move your finger back to the Fortress of Antonia.	Herod grew tired of him and sent him back to Pilate at the Fortress of Antonia.
	Pilate then showed Jesus to the crowd. There was a tradition to release a prisoner at the time of the Passover. Pilate asked the crowd if he should release Jesus or Barabbas. They shouted, "Barabbas!"
	The soldiers prepared Jesus to be crucified. They then took him through the streets to Golgotha, which means "the place of the skull", where they hung him on the cross and he died.
Trace the route from the Fortress of Antonia to Golgotha, where you have already placed the marker to show the site of the crucifixion and the tomb. The actual site is uncertain, but it was outside the wall of the city to the northwest.	People still walk along these streets to remember Jesus and pray. Today they move from a school, where the Roman fortress used to be, along the Via Dolorosa, the Street of Sadness, to the Church of the Holy Sepulchre.
	After Jesus died, the disciples took him down from the cross and placed him a tomb nearby, given by Joseph of Arimathea.
	A great stone was rolled in front of the opening to close it like a locked door.
	On Saturday everything was quiet
	On Sunday the women had the courage to go to the tomb just to be close to Jesus. When they got there, they found the stone had been rolled away and discovered that somehow he was still with them, as he is with us today.
Sit back and take a deep breath. This shows that the story is over and that it is time for the wondering to begin.	
Wait a moment and then begin the wondering.	I wonder what part you like best?
	I wonder what part is the most important?
	I wonder what part is about you, or where are you in the story?
	I wonder if there is anything we could leave out and still have all the story we need?

MOVEMENTS

Wait until the wondering begins to lose its energy and then sit back for a moment of reflection. You then put everything into the tray and place it back on the shelf.

It is now time to help the children get out their work.

WORDS

I wonder what we can do in our church during Holy Week to remember this?

I wonder if there is more we can do to mark this special week?

➡ I wonder what you would like to make your work today?

LESSON 6

MARY, THE MOTHER OF JESUS

LESSON NOTES

FOCUS: MARY, THE MOTHER OF JESUS (LUKE 1:26–34, LUKE 2:1–20, MATTHEW 1:18–25, LUKE 2:21–52, LUKE 4:16–30, JOHN 2:1–12, MATTHEW 12:46–50, JOHN 19:25–27)

- SACRED STORY
- EXTENSION OF "THE GREATEST PARABLE" AND "FACES OF EASTER, PART 1"

THE MATERIAL

- LOCATION: NEW TESTAMENT SACRED STORY SHELF, SECOND SHELF, UNDER THE GREATEST PARABLE
- PIECES: ANGEL PLAQUE, WOODEN CHRIST CHILD IN A MANGER, CRUCIFIX, TOMB, WOODEN FIRE IMAGE, SILK FORGET-ME-NOTS
- UNDERLAY: STRIP OF BLUE FELT

BACKGROUND

God chose Mary to be the Mother of God when she was a young teenager. Joseph and Mary raised the baby and Mary was present during Jesus' life and death. Legends beginning about the second century tell us that her mother's name was Anne and her father's name was Joachim. Mary's story parallels the stories of divine intervention in the birth of Isaac to Sarah, and Samuel to Hannah (a Hebrew form of Anne).

NOTES ON THE MATERIAL

This lesson is kept in a wooden tray, like other stories that are extensions of Core stories. The story icon is an image of Mary holding the infant Jesus. The underlay is a strip of blue felt. Each object in the story is approximately the same size (no more than 4 inches high and wide). The story calls for the following objects: an angel image, a wooden Christ child in a manger (like in "The Holy Family"), a scroll of Isaiah (like in "The Synagogue and the Upper Room"), a crucifix, an empty tomb, a red flame made of wood to represent the Holy Spirit, and silk forget-me-nots. The control for the lesson is placed in the bottom of the tray for the children to use to check their work to be sure that the sequence of the story is right, because when you change the sequence, you change the story.

SPECIAL NOTES

This story can be told any time during the church year, but is especially appropriate during the seasons of Advent or Lent.

WHERE TO FIND MATERIALS

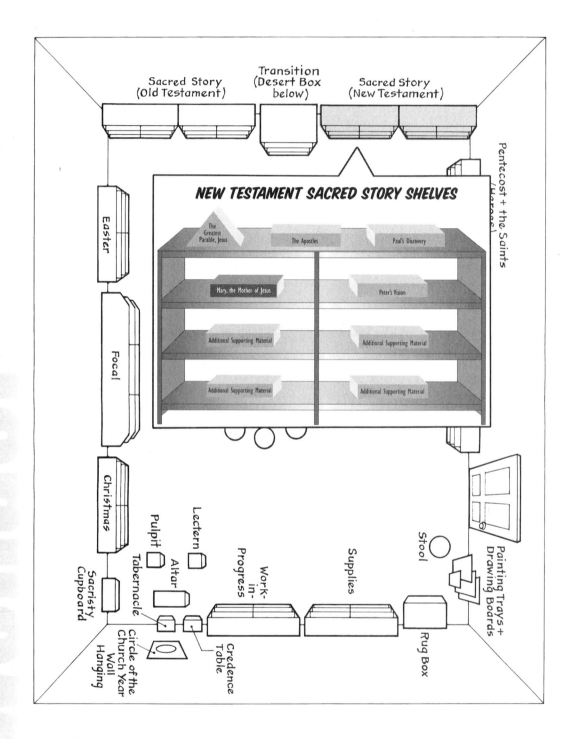

MOVEMENTS	WORDS

<table>
<tr><td>Move slowly with deliberation to the shelf where the material waits.</td><td>Watch. Watch where I go.</td></tr>
<tr><td>Pick up the tray containing the materials and return to the circle. You may need to say, depending on the day:</td><td>Everyone needs to be ready.</td></tr>
<tr><td>Remove the underlay from the tray. Unroll it from your right to left, leaving enough room for the first object to be placed on it. (Continue to unroll the underlay a little at a time, as each subsequent object is laid on it.)</td><td></td></tr>
<tr><td></td><td>When Mary was a little girl, she wondered what it would be like when she was all grown up. The years went by and one day something happened that no one could explain.</td></tr>
<tr><td>Object #1: angel image</td><td>The angel Gabriel came to her and said, "God has chosen you to be the Mother of God."
But what did that mean?
She was about to be married to a wonderful man, who was a carpenter in Nazareth.
His name was Joseph.</td></tr>
<tr><td>Object #2: the baby Jesus in a manger</td><td>Then, the angel came to Joseph and said that Mary was going to have a baby, and that the baby was God.
Now Joseph was confused, too.
But Joseph and Mary were married anyway, and the baby was born. They named him Jesus.

Many more things happened that were hard to understand. When Jesus was just eight days old they took him to the Temple in Jerusalem to present him to God, as was the custom.
Old Simeon was there waiting.
When he saw Jesus he said something like this, "Now I can die. I have seen the Messiah."

When Jesus was about twelve, Mary and Joseph lost him in Jerusalem, but found him in the Temple. He said, "Didn't you know that I would be in my father's house?" But Joseph's house was in Nazareth, where the carpenter's shop was. The boy became more confusing as he grew to be a man.</td></tr>
</table>

MOVEMENTS	WORDS
Object #3: the Scroll of Isaiah	When he began to teach, he returned to his home synagogue and read from the scroll of Isaiah about the coming of the Messiah. He then said that he was the One. Mary must have remembered the angel Gabriel, but the people of Nazareth were angry. They tried to throw him off a cliff.
	At a wedding he changed the water into wine and another time Mary and his brothers came to see him when he was teaching. He said that those who followed him were his family, not them. Now his brothers were confused, too.
Object #4: the crucifix	Then Jesus went to Jerusalem for the last time, and Mary was there. When they put him on the cross, she stood watching, probably standing near John. People have written beautiful and sad music about this. It is called the *Stabat Mater*, because the Mother was just standing there. What was she thinking?
	Then, Jesus lifted his head and spoke to her. "Woman, behold your son!" He then said to a disciple, "Behold, your mother!" The disciple, who was probably John, took her into his own home and cared for her in her old age.
	When they took Jesus down from the cross, Mary was still there. Sometimes you will see a statue or a painting of Mary holding Jesus in her lap. It is called a *Pieta*, which means pity and a kind devotion. That is how she felt.
Object #5: the empty tomb	The next day was very quiet and empty for Mary. Then, on Sunday, the first Easter, she and the other women walked slowly back to the place where Jesus had been put in the tomb. She needed to be close to him. They found that the stone had been rolled away and that somehow Jesus was still with them, as he is with us today.
Object #6: the flames	When the disciples returned from Mount Olivet after Jesus ascended, Mary and his brothers were with them. The waited in the upper room with the others. Mary was there a week later when the sound of the mighty wind filled the room and the Holy Spirit came like fire.
	No one knows when Mary died or was buried, but she was truly the Mother of God. When she was all grown up, she kept on growing. People still feel close to her. They name churches after her and make pilgrimages to places where she seems especially close.

MOVEMENTS

WORDS

Object #7: The blue, silk forget-me-nots ➡ This is one of those stories, then, that never ends, so instead of ending it we will put down some of Mary's flowers.
They are called forget-me-nots.
She will never be forgotten.

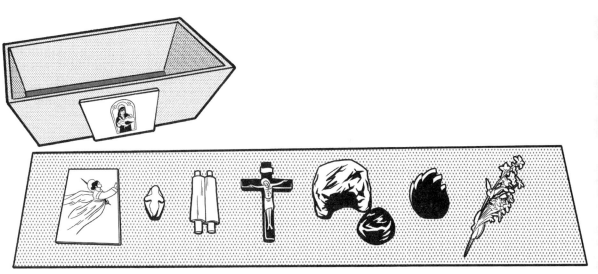

COMPLETE LAYOUT OF THE STORY OF MARY, THE MOTHER OF JESUS

I wonder what part of this story you liked the best?

I wonder what part of this story is the most important?

I wonder what part is about you, or is especially for you?

I wonder if we can leave out any of the story and still have all that we need?

Name each object and say a brief word about it as you place it back on the tray. For example: "Here is the red flame that reminds us that Mary was there when the Holy Spirit came." Roll up the underlay carefully and place it on the tray, then return the story to its place on the shelf.

Return to the circle and begin to guide ➡ I wonder what you would like to make your work today?
the children as they choose their work.

LESSON 7

KNOWING JESUS IN A NEW WAY, PART 1: KNOWN IN ABSENCE

LESSON NOTES

FOCUS: KNOWN IN ABSENCE (MARK 16:1-7, MATTHEW 28:1-8, LUKE 24:1-11, JOHN 20:1-10)

- LITURGICAL ACTION
- CORE PRESENTATION

THE MATERIAL

- LOCATION: THE MYSTERY OF PENTECOST SHELF, TOP SHELF—FIRST LESSON
- PIECES: 6 PLAQUES ILLUSTRATED WITH THE RESURRECTION APPEARANCES OF JESUS, 1 PLAQUE ILLUSTRATED WITH THE GIFT OF THE HOLY SPIRIT AT PENTECOST, A STAND TO HOLD ALL 7 PLAQUES
- UNDERLAY: 6 WHITE PANELS AND 1 RED PANEL SEPARATED BY NARROW, GOLD PIECES OF WOOD

BACKGROUND

The season of Easter (Eastertide) extends the experience of Easter Sunday for six weeks, but it also helps prepare for the coming of the Mystery of Pentecost. This period is a transition between Jesus' earthly ministry and the coming of the Holy Spirit. It is a time when the disciples and others began to know Jesus in a new way. He is neither simply human nor simply spiritual. He is completely both in a way that is anything but simple.

Jesus' appearances have fascinated people from the disciples, to the opponents of the early Christians, to the present. What did they experience? Clearly it was something very powerful. Paul was an opponent of the Followers of the Way, yet his experience of Jesus after the Resurrection completely changed his life. It turned him around and toward what would later be called "Christian."

Paul provided us with the earliest written list of appearances still available to us. It can be found in what we today call his "first" letter to the church at Corinth (I Corinthians 15:3 – 11). His list began with Cephas, which means "Peter" in Aramaic. It continues with the disciples and then "more than five hundred …most …still alive." James was listed next. He is only the second person Paul specifically named as a participant in this experience in addition to himself, "the least of the apostles." Our task here, however, is not to explain or analyze. It is to tell the story, drawing on the season of Eastertide to guide us by its structure, as we make our way toward Pentecost and the coming of the Holy Spirit in the lives of the disciples and in our own.

This is not to say that the time, place, and identity of those experiencing Jesus in this new way and related matters are not interesting and significant. They are. This is only to say that such talk would shift the emphasis in this introduction from guiding the storytelling to an analysis of the texts and their context, which is a very different kind of communication. Such an analysis can be saved for another time. For now it is enough to say that the scriptural texts each presentation draws on in this series are indicated at the beginning of each lesson.

Our focus here is on Jesus' followers, as they experienced the fearful wonder and astonishment of this transition time. It was a vast adjustment to learn how to know Jesus in this new way. Furthermore, in all of the appearances there is at least an implied call to mission. The disciples were commissioned to spread the good news of the reality they experienced during the transition and in Pentecost. There was no precedent for this. They were called to help God create a new and unknown world! Such a vocation was overwhelming for them, as it is for us today, but we, at least, have this story to guide us. They did not. They had to create God's creation anew, as we must also do in our own time guided by Eastertide and Pentecost.

NOTES ON THE MATERIAL

Everything you need for this presentation is located on the Pentecost Shelf. The rack, sitting on the top shelf, holds both the underlay and the seven images depicting the six appearances and Pentecost. The images stand up in this rack so the children can see the art and be drawn to it.

This presentation is like the "Faces of Easter" although it begins where the "Faces" ends. The underlay is unrolled back toward the storyteller from the middle of the circle rather than away from the storyteller. In the "Faces" the storyteller helps give birth to the narrative of the One who becomes Easter. In this lesson the storyteller is reborn in narrative by the loss, astonishment, and longing of the disciples, as they move inward to receive the Holy Spirit in Pentecost.

This lesson ends like "Faces" with a change of color. The change is from white to red and marks the shift from preparation encounters to the Mystery of Pentecost itself. The moving out in the "Faces of Easter" returns inward with the Pentecost lesson. It marks the new reality that the disciples learned to know and trust. God's elusive presence is not only beyond in the creation and beside us as Jesus, the redemptive companion of the Gospels, but is also within to motivate and sustain us to move on in our journey. The divinity and humanity of Jesus, a coincidence of opposites, is clarified experientially by this process to provide a new way to conceive of what is really good and true and beautiful in life and death.

The rhythm of moving out and within again requires two different kinds of art. In "Faces" the art shows the changing face of the One who is Easter, drawing on the theme of faces in the Old and New Testaments, such as how the face of Moses glowed when he emerged from the Tabernacle. It also draws on the way of saying "intimate presence" in Hebrew with the lovely phrase "face to face." In this series of lessons, however, Jesus' presence is suggested by the faces of the disciples. The children are invited into the perplexity and wonder of the disciples as they see Jesus in this new way. It is the space between them and Jesus that the children are invited to enter, so the centuries can dissolve, enabling the children to be there, as Jesus is here.

SPECIAL NOTES

In conclusion there is an important similarity between this lesson and the "Faces of Easter" that needs special emphasis. At the end of each presentation during the six Sundays of Eastertide the children are invited to choose materials from around the room that will help tell more of the story or that their intuition tells them need to be placed next to each picture, even if they can't articulate why.

For example, when you tell the story of the women at the empty tomb, one child might bring the Mary figure from "The Holy Family" on the altar/focal shelf to put beside the image. Another child might bring the crucifixion marker from "Jesus and Jerusalem" or the whole box of crosses from the enrichment lesson about crosses to put beside the tile. Be open to the surprising connections children make, as they explore the meaning embodied in the stories of the disciples' encounters with the risen Christ. There is much to be learned from them as we make this journey together in Godly Play.

WHERE TO FIND THE MATERIAL

As we have said, the seven parts to the lesson "Knowing Jesus in a New Way" are found on the top shelf of the Pentecost shelf unit. The classroom map suggests where this might be, but your Godly Play room may not be as fully developed as this one or look exactly like it. You will need to find a way to be creative, following the principles of how the room is laid out. For example, your Godly Play room may not be a perfect rectangle. What do you do then? You do the best you can.

WHERE TO FIND MATERIALS

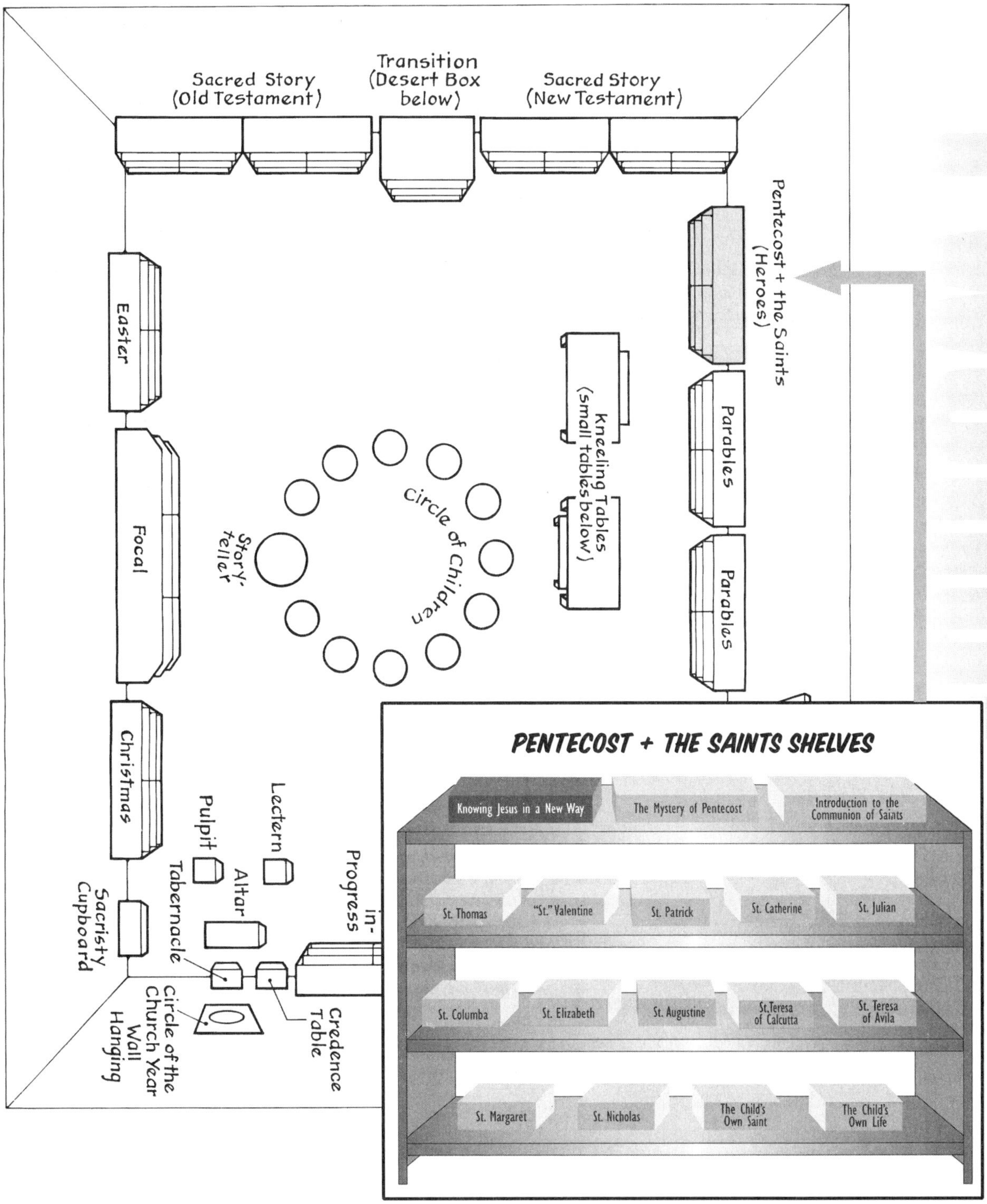

Transition (Desert Box below)
Sacred Story (Old Testament)
Sacred Story (New Testament)
Pentecost + the Saints (Heroes)
Easter
Focal
Christmas
Sacristy Cupboard
Kneeling Tables (small tables below)
Parables
Parables
Circle of Children
Story-teller
Lectern
Pulpit
Altar
Tabernacle
in-Progress
Circle of the Church Year Wall Hanging
Credence Table
PENTECOST + THE SAINTS SHELVES
Knowing Jesus in a New Way
The Mystery of Pentecost
Introduction to the Communion of Saints
St. Thomas
"St." Valentine
St. Patrick
St. Catherine
St. Julian
St. Columba
St. Elizabeth
St. Augustine
St. Teresa of Calcutta
St. Teresa of Avila
St. Margaret
St. Nicholas
The Child's Own Saint
The Child's Own Life

MOVEMENTS	WORDS
When the children are ready, go and get the material from the shelf.	Watch where I go, so you will always know where to get this lesson in case you want to work on it by yourself or with friends.
Unroll the underlay toward you from the middle of the circle so that the end of the first white section can be seen in the center of the circle.	
Take the first image (the women at the tomb) from the stand and tell the story while holding it front of you.	On the first day of knowing Jesus in a new way, the women went to the tomb. There were three "Marys"—among others. Mary Magdalene seemed to lead the way, and there was Mary, the mother of James, and Mary, the mother of Jesus. Mary Magdalene was not a mother. She was a good and strong friend. They carried spices with them to finish the burial and wondered how they would get inside. When they came to the tomb, the stone had been rolled away, so they looked in. What they saw was nothing, nothing but the white, linen cloth that had covered his body.
Touch the figure of Mary looking inside and then sweep your hand around the linen cloth.	They went back to tell the others, but most did not believe them. Peter, being Peter, jumped up and ran to the tomb. Some say John ran too and got there first. He waited for Peter and they went in together. They could feel his presence in the absence, but Jesus was gone, gone, truly gone. Mary Magdalene came up and stood outside weeping. Peter and John went back, but Mary stayed. "Woman, why are you weeping?" Through her tears she saw two men, dressed in white. "Jesus has gone on. Tell the disciples to meet him in Galilee." "Woman, why are you weeping," another voice asked. She turned and saw someone, who must have been the gardener. "Tell me where they have taken him. I will go and take him away." "Mary." This time he said her name and she knew it was he.

MOVEMENTS

WORDS

Mary must have stepped forward, because Jesus said, "No. You cannot hold me. I have risen but not yet ascended." Then he was gone. Mary went back to tell the others.

When you have enjoyed for a moment the presence of Jesus in the tomb's emptiness, lay the image on the underlay, facing the children.

KNOWN IN ABSENCE (VIEW FROM THE CHILDREN'S PERSPECTIVE)

Begin to go around the circle, asking each child if he or she would like to bring something to put by the image on the underlay. Some children may not be able to think of anything or may be too shy to do this, so move on if it looks as if they are stuck. You can come back to them later. If they are still stuck, that is okay.

Many children learn by watching as well as by doing and they may be deeply considering this, despite staying still.

Now I wonder if there is anything in this room that you can bring and put beside this picture to help us tell more about this part of the story? Is there something that just calls to you and seems like it needs to be there? Look around and see.

I will go around the circle and ask each one of you if you would like to go and get something to put beside this image to show more about it.

I wonder

MOVEMENTS

Sometimes children get up, wander for a moment and bring something at random, without knowing why. That's also okay. Be amazed—which is easy—and wonder with them how this is really relevant. Everything in the room is connected in some way, but it is sometimes up to the storyteller to put that into a few words with wonder. Enjoy the items that the children bring to help tell the story.

When you have had time to enjoy the entire layout, invite children, one at a time, to return their chosen materials to the correct shelves.

Then, put the image back on the stand beside you, roll up the underlay, place it back on the stand, and return the lesson to the Pentecost shelf.

When everything is back in its place, you can begin to help children, one at a time, to choose their work.

WORDS

I don't know what you are going to get.
You are the only one in the world who knows that. If you don't feel like getting something, that's okay. Just enjoy what we make together. You are still part of what we make.

I wonder what you would like to make your work today?

LESSON 8

KNOWING JESUS IN A NEW WAY, PART 2: KNOWN IN THE BREAKING OF BREAD

LESSON NOTES

FOCUS: KNOWN IN THE BREAKING OF BREAD (LUKE 24:13-35)

- LITURGICAL ACTION
- CORE PRESENTATION

THE MATERIAL

- LOCATION: THE MYSTERY OF PENTECOST SHELF, TOP SHELF—FIRST LESSON
- PIECES: 6 PLAQUES ILLUSTRATED WITH THE RESURRECTION APPEARANCES OF JESUS, 1 PLAQUE ILLUSTRATED WITH THE GIFT OF THE HOLY SPIRIT AT PENTECOST, A STAND TO HOLD THE 7 PLAQUES
- UNDERLAY: 6 WHITE PANELS AND 1 RED PANEL SEPARATED BY NARROW, GOLD PIECES OF WOOD

BACKGROUND

The season of Easter (Eastertide) extends the experience of Easter Sunday for six weeks, but it also helps prepare for the coming of the Mystery of Pentecost. This period is a transition between Jesus' earthly ministry and the coming of the Holy Spirit. It is a time when the disciples and others began to know Jesus in a new way. He is neither simply human nor simply spiritual. He is completely both in a way that is anything but simple.

Jesus' appearances have fascinated people from the disciples, to the opponents of the early Christians, to the present. What did they experience? Clearly it was something very powerful. Paul was an opponent of the Followers of the Way, yet his experience of Jesus after the Resurrection completely changed his life. It turned him around and toward what would later be called "Christian."

Paul provided us with the earliest written list of appearances still available to us. It can be found in what we today call his "first" letter to the church at Corinth (I Corinthians 15:3 – 11). His list began with Cephas, which means "Peter" in Aramaic. It continues with the disciples and then "more than five hundred …most …still alive." James was listed next. He is only the second person Paul specifically named as a participant in this experience in addition to himself, "the least of the apostles." Our task here, however, is not to explain or analyze. It is to tell the story, drawing on the season of

Eastertide to guide us by its structure, as we make our way toward Pentecost and the coming of the Holy Spirit in the lives of the disciples and in our own.

This is not to say that the time, place, and identity of those experiencing Jesus in this new way and related matters are not interesting and significant. They are. This is only to say that such talk would shift the emphasis in this introduction from guiding the storytelling to an analysis of the texts and their context, which is a very different kind of communication. Such an analysis can be saved for another time. For now it is enough to say that the scriptural texts each presentation draws on in this series are indicated at the beginning of each lesson.

Our focus here is on Jesus' followers, as they experienced the fearful wonder and astonishment of this transition time. It was a vast adjustment to learn how to know Jesus in this new way. Furthermore, in all of the appearances there is at least an implied call to mission. The disciples were commissioned to spread the good news of the reality they experienced during the transition and in Pentecost. There was no precedent for this. They were called to help God create a new and unknown world! Such a vocation was overwhelming for them, as it is for us today, but we, at least, have this story to guide us. They did not. They had to create God's creation anew, as we must also do in our own time guided by Eastertide and Pentecost.

NOTES ON THE MATERIAL

Everything you need for this presentation is located on the Pentecost Shelf. The rack, sitting on the top shelf, holds both the underlay and the seven images depicting the six appearances and Pentecost. The images stand up in this rack so the children can see the art and be drawn to it.

This presentation is like the "Faces of Easter" although it begins where the "Faces" ends. The underlay is unrolled back toward the storyteller from the middle of the circle rather than away from the storyteller. In the "Faces" the storyteller helps give birth to the narrative of the One who becomes Easter. In this lesson the storyteller is reborn in narrative by the loss, astonishment, and longing of the disciples, as they move inward to receive the Holy Spirit in Pentecost.

This lesson ends like "Faces" with a change of color. The change is from white to red and marks the shift from preparation encounters to the Mystery of Pentecost itself. The moving out in the "Faces of Easter" returns inward with the Pentecost lesson. It marks the new reality that the disciples learned to know and trust. God's elusive presence is not only beyond in the creation and beside us as Jesus, the redemptive companion of the Gospels, but is also within to motivate and sustain us to move on in our journey. The divinity and humanity of Jesus, a coincidence of opposites, is clarified experientially by this process to provide a new way to conceive of what is really good and true and beautiful in life and death.

The rhythm of moving out and within again requires two different kinds of art. In "Faces" the art shows the changing face of the One who is Easter, drawing on the theme of faces in the Old and New Testaments, such as how the face of Moses glowed when he emerged from the Tabernacle. It also draws on the way of saying "intimate presence" in Hebrew with the lovely phrase "face to face." In this series of lessons, however, Jesus' presence is suggested by the faces of the disciples. The children are invited into the perplexity and wonder of the disciples as they see Jesus in this new way. It is the space between them and Jesus that the children are invited to enter, so the centuries can dissolve, enabling the children to be there, as Jesus is here.

SPECIAL NOTES

In conclusion there is an important similarity between this lesson and the "Faces of Easter" that needs special emphasis. At the end of each presentation during the six Sundays of Eastertide the children are invited to choose materials from around the room that will help tell more of the story or that their intuition tells them need to be placed next to each picture, even if they can't articulate why.

For example, when you tell the story of the women at the empty tomb, one child might bring the Mary figure from "The Holy Family" on the altar/focal shelf to put beside the image. Another child might bring the crucifixion marker from "Jesus and Jerusalem" or the whole box of crosses from the enrichment lesson about crosses to put beside the tile. Be open to the surprising connections children make, as they explore the meaning embodied in the stories of the disciples' encounters with the risen Christ. There is much to be learned from them as we make this journey together in Godly Play.

WHERE TO FIND THE MATERIAL

As we have said, the seven parts to the lesson "Knowing Jesus in a New Way" are found on the top shelf of the Pentecost shelf unit. The classroom map suggests where this might be, but your Godly Play room may not be as fully developed as this one or look exactly like it. You will need to find a way to be creative, following the principles of how the room is laid out. For example, your Godly Play room may not be a perfect rectangle. What do you do then? You do the best you can.

WHERE TO FIND MATERIALS

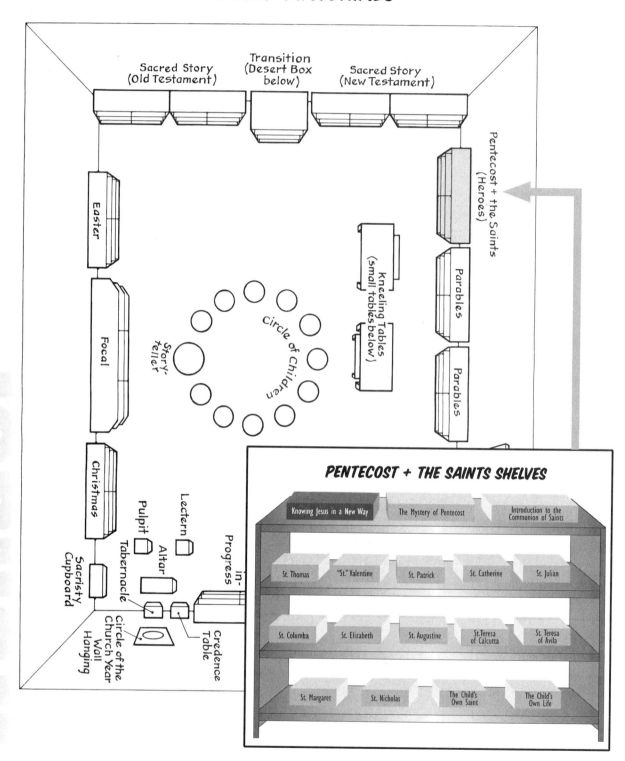

Sacred Story (Old Testament)

Transition (Desert Box below)

Sacred Story (New Testament)

Easter

Focal

Christmas

Pentecost + the Saints (Heroes)

Parables

Parables

Kneeling Tables (small tables below)

Story-teller

Circle of Children

Lectern

Pulpit

Altar

Tabernacle

Sacristy Cupboard

in-Progress

Credence Table

Circle of the Church Year Wall Hanging

PENTECOST + THE SAINTS SHELVES

Knowing Jesus in a New Way | The Mystery of Pentecost | Introduction to the Communion of Saints

St. Thomas | "St." Valentine | St. Patrick | St. Catherine | St. Julian

St. Columba | St. Elizabeth | St. Augustine | St. Teresa of Calcutta | St. Teresa of Avila

St. Margaret | St. Nicholas | The Child's Own Saint | The Child's Own Life

I wonder

MOVEMENTS	WORDS
When the children are ready, go and get the material from the shelf. ⟶	Watch where I go to get the lesson for today.
Unroll the underlay toward you to the end of the first white section. Summarize the first image (the women at the tomb) while holding it in front of you and then place it on the underlay.	
Unroll the underlay to the end of second ⟶ *white section and tell the story while holding the second image (Jesus and two of his disciples breaking bread) in front of you.*	On the second Sunday in the season of Easter we remember how in the afternoon of the first Easter, two of Jesus' followers made their way slowly toward Emmaus, some seven miles from Jerusalem.

They must have been shaking their heads in wonder as they walked and talked of what had happened.
The cross...The empty tomb...
What did it mean?

A stranger joined them.
They didn't really pay much attention until he asked, "What are you talking about?"

"Are you the only one in Jerusalem who has not heard what has taken place these last three days?"

"What happened?"

"The cross. The empty tomb.
There has been so much!"

"You are foolish and slow of heart. Listen." He opened the scriptures to them.

"Do you remember how we were trapped in Egypt and Moses led us out through the water into freedom? Do you remember how we were trapped in our freedom in the desert and God gave Moses the Ten Commandments to guide us? Do you remember how we were trapped in exile and the prophets said a child would lead us and that someone would come to suffer and die so we might be really alive?"

MOVEMENTS	WORDS
	By this time they were in the village of Emmaus. The miles had passed quickly as the stranger talked. He was about to go on when the two asked him to stay and he did.
Touch the bread being given in the picture. ➠	When they sat at supper in the inn, the stranger took a piece of bread. He gave thanks to God for it and broke it. He then shared it with the two. That was when they knew who he was, but in that moment he was gone.
Circle your hand around the table and the two men. ➠	They sat at the table for a time, talking. Now they knew why their hearts had burned within as they walked with him on the road. They got up slowly and hurried back to Jerusalem to tell the rest that he had been made known to them in the breaking of bread.

When you have felt, for a moment, the presence of Jesus to the disciples in breaking of the bread, put the image down on the underlay, facing the children.

ADDING KNOWN IN THE BREAKING OF BREAD (VIEW FROM THE CHILDREN'S PERSPECTIVE)

MOVEMENTS

Begin to go around the circle, asking each child if he or she would like to bring something to put by the image on the underlay. Some children may not be able to think of anything or may be too shy to do this, so move on if it looks as if they are stuck. You can come back to them later. If they are still stuck, that is okay.

Many children learn by watching as well as by doing and they may be deeply considering this, despite staying still.

Sometimes children get up, wander for a moment and bring something at random, without knowing why. That's also okay. Be amazed—which is easy—and wonder with them how this is really relevant. Everything in the room is connected in some way, but it is sometimes up to the storyteller to put that into a few words with wonder. Enjoy the items that the children bring to help tell the story.

When you have had time to enjoy the entire layout, invite children, one at a time, to return their chosen materials to the correct shelves.

Then, put the images back on the stand beside you, roll up the underlay, place it back on the stand, and return the lesson to the Pentecost shelf.

When everything is back in its place, you can begin to help children, one at a time, to choose their work.

WORDS

Now I wonder if there is anything in this room that you can bring and put beside this picture to help us tell more about this part of the story? Is there something that just calls to you and seems like it needs to be there? Look around and see.

I will go around the circle and ask each one of you if you would like to go and get something to put beside this image to show more about it.

I don't know what you are going to get.

You are the only one in the world who knows that. If you don't feel like getting something, that's okay. Just enjoy what we make together. You are still part of what we make.

I wonder what you would like to make your work today?

LESSON 9

KNOWING JESUS IN A NEW WAY, PART 3: KNOWN IN DOUBT

LESSON NOTES

FOCUS: KNOWN IN DOUBT (LUKE 20:19-29)

- ● LITURGICAL ACTION
- ● CORE PRESENTATION

THE MATERIAL

- ● LOCATION: THE MYSTERY OF PENTECOST SHELF, TOP SHELF—FIRST LESSON
- ● PIECES: 6 PLAQUES ILLUSTRATED WITH THE RESURRECTION APPEARANCES OF JESUS, 1 PLAQUE ILLUSTRATED WITH THE GIFT OF THE HOLY SPIRIT AT PENTECOST, A STAND TO HOLD THE 7 PLAQUES
- ● UNDERLAY: 6 WHITE PANELS AND 1 RED PANEL SEPARATED BY NARROW, GOLD PIECES OF WOOD

BACKGROUND

The season of Easter (Eastertide) extends the experience of Easter Sunday for six weeks, but it also helps prepare for the coming of the Mystery of Pentecost. This period is a transition between Jesus' earthly ministry and the coming of the Holy Spirit. It is a time when the disciples and others began to know Jesus in a new way. He is neither simply human nor simply spiritual. He is completely both in a way that is anything but simple.

Jesus' appearances have fascinated people from the disciples, to the opponents of the early Christians, to the present. What did they experience? Clearly it was something very powerful. Paul was an opponent of the Followers of the Way, yet his experience of Jesus after the Resurrection completely changed his life. It turned him around and toward what would later be called "Christian."

Paul provided us with the earliest written list of appearances still available to us. It can be found in what we today call his "first" letter to the church at Corinth (I Corinthians 15:3 – 11). His list began with Cephas, which means "Peter" in Aramaic. It continues with the disciples and then "more than five hundred …most …still alive." James was listed next. He is only the second person Paul specifically named as a participant in this experience in addition to himself, "the least of the apostles." Our task here, however, is not to explain or analyze. It is to tell the story, drawing on the season of Eastertide to guide us by its structure, as we make our way toward Pentecost and the coming of the Holy Spirit in the lives of the disciples and in our own.

This is not to say that the time, place, and identity of those experiencing Jesus in this new way and related matters are not interesting and significant. They are. This is only to say that such talk would shift the emphasis in this introduction from guiding the storytelling to an analysis of the texts and their context, which is a very different kind of communication. Such an analysis can be saved for another time. For now it is enough to say that the scriptural texts each presentation draws on in this series are indicated at the beginning of each lesson.

Our focus here is on Jesus' followers, as they experienced the fearful wonder and astonishment of this transition time. It was a vast adjustment to learn how to know Jesus in this new way. Furthermore, in all of the appearances there is at least an implied call to mission. The disciples were commissioned to spread the good news of the reality they experienced during the transition and in Pentecost. There was no precedent for this. They were called to help God create a new and unknown world! Such a vocation was overwhelming for them, as it is for us today, but we, at least, have this story to guide us. They did not. They had to create God's creation anew, as we must also do in our own time guided by Eastertide and Pentecost.

NOTES ON THE MATERIAL

Everything you need for this presentation is located on the Pentecost Shelf. The rack, sitting on the top shelf, holds both the underlay and the seven images depicting the six appearances and Pentecost. The images stand up in this rack so the children can see the art and be drawn to it.

This presentation is like the "Faces of Easter" although it begins where the "Faces" ends. The underlay is unrolled back toward the storyteller from the middle of the circle rather than away from the storyteller. In the "Faces" the storyteller helps give birth to the narrative of the One who becomes Easter. In this lesson the storyteller is reborn in narrative by the loss, astonishment, and longing of the disciples, as they move inward to receive the Holy Spirit in Pentecost.

This lesson ends like "Faces" with a change of color. The change is from white to red and marks the shift from preparation encounters to the Mystery of Pentecost itself. The moving out in the "Faces of Easter" returns inward with the Pentecost lesson. It marks the new reality that the disciples learned to know and trust. God's elusive presence is not only beyond in the creation and beside us as Jesus, the redemptive companion of the Gospels, but is also within to motivate and sustain us to move on in our journey. The divinity and humanity of Jesus, a coincidence of opposites, is clarified experientially by this process to provide a new way to conceive of what is really good and true and beautiful in life and death.

The rhythm of moving out and within again requires two different kinds of art. In "Faces" the art shows the changing face of the One who is Easter, drawing on the theme of faces in the Old and New Testaments, such as how the face of Moses glowed when he emerged from the Tabernacle. It also draws on the way of saying "intimate presence" in Hebrew with the lovely phrase "face to face." In this series of lessons, however, Jesus' presence is suggested by the faces of the disciples. The children are invited into the perplexity and wonder of the disciples as they see Jesus in this new way. It is the space between them and Jesus that the children are invited to enter, so the centuries can dissolve, enabling the children to be there, as Jesus is here.

SPECIAL NOTES

In conclusion there is an important similarity between this lesson and the "Faces of Easter" that needs special emphasis. At the end of each presentation during the six Sundays of Eastertide the children are invited to choose materials from around the room that will help tell more of the story or that their intuition tells them need to be placed next to each picture, even if they can't articulate why.

For example, when you tell the story of the women at the empty tomb, one child might bring the Mary figure from "The Holy Family" on the altar/focal shelf to put beside the image. Another child might bring the three crosses from "Jesus and Jerusalem" or the whole box of crosses from the enrichment lesson about crosses to put beside the tile. Be open to the surprising connections children make, as they explore the meaning embodied in the stories of the disciples' encounters with the risen Christ. There is much to be learned from them as we make this journey together in Godly Play.

WHERE TO FIND THE MATERIAL

As we have said, the seven parts to the lesson "Knowing Jesus in a New Way" are found on the top shelf of the Pentecost shelf unit. The classroom map suggests where this might be, but your Godly Play room may not be as fully developed as this one or look exactly like it. You will need to find a way to be creative, following the principles of how the room is laid out. For example, your Godly Play room may not be a perfect rectangle. What do you do then? You do the best you can.

WHERE TO FIND MATERIALS

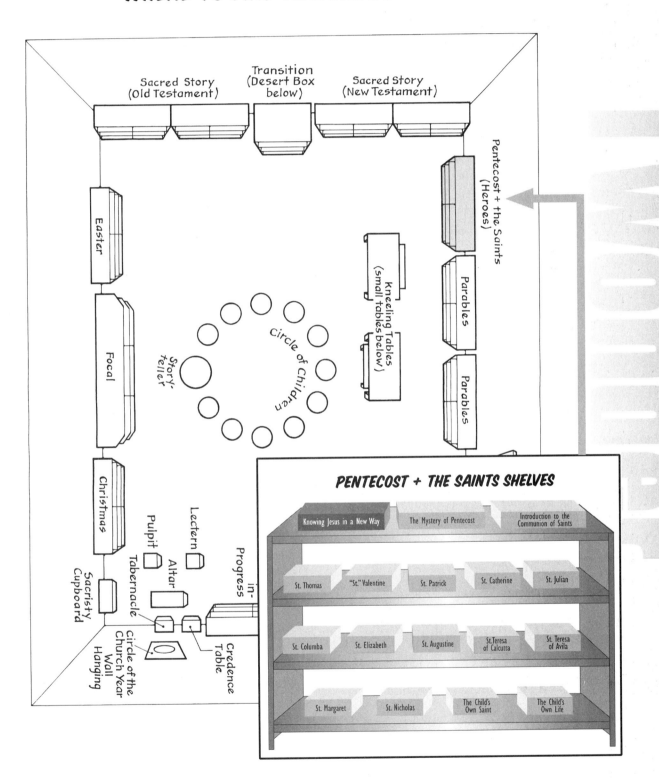

Sacred Story (Old Testament)

Transition (Desert Box below)

Sacred Story (New Testament)

Pentecost + the Saints (Heroes)

Easter

Focal

Christmas

Story-teller

Circle of Children

Kneeling Tables (small tables below)

Parables

Parables

in-Progress

Pulpit

Lectern

Altar

Tabernacle

Sacristy Cupboard

circle of the Church Year Wall Hanging

Credence Table

PENTECOST + THE SAINTS SHELVES

Knowing Jesus in a New Way | The Mystery of Pentecost | Introduction to the Communion of Saints

St. Thomas | "St." Valentine | St. Patrick | St. Catherine | St. Julian

St. Columba | St. Elizabeth | St. Augustine | St. Teresa of Calcutta | St. Teresa of Avila

St. Margaret | St. Nicholas | The Child's Own Saint | The Child's Own Life

MOVEMENTS

WORDS

When the children are ready, go and get the material from the shelf. ➧ Watch where I go to get the lesson for today.

Unroll the underlay toward you to the end of the first white section. Summarize the first image (the women at the tomb) while holding it in front of you and then place it on the underlay.

Unroll the underlay to the end of second white section. Summarize the second image (Jesus and two of his followers breaking bread) while holding it in front of you and then place it on the underlay.

Unroll the underlay to the end of the third white section and tell the story while holding the third image (Thomas kneeling before Jesus) in front of you. ➧ On the third Sunday in the season of Easter we remember how one night it was dark in Jerusalem when the disciples gathered in a room with the doors shut.

They were afraid that the soldiers would come and take them, like they had taken Jesus.

Someone said, "Peace be with you."
They looked and it was He.

At first they thought it was a ghost, but then he talked with them.

They saw his wounds. He ate a piece of fish and opened the scriptures as he had on the road to Emmaus.

Finally, he said again, "Peace be with you" and was gone.

Thomas had been away that night. When they told him the next day what had happened he did not believe them.
He had doubt in his bones. "I won't believe until I can touch his wounds."

And why wouldn't he have some doubt? Their minds were stretching, stretching, stretching to be big enough to know Jesus in this new way.

MOVEMENTS

WORDS

Eight days passed. The disciples again gathered in the room with the doors shut. This time Thomas was there.
A voice said "Peace be with you."
It was he and this time he went right up to Thomas and held out his hand.

Point to Jesus' hand in the image.

"Touch me."
All Thomas could do was fall on his knees.
"My Lord and my God."

Move your hand down over the picture and let your hand fall away. Circle Thomas' face lightly with your finger.

Jesus looked at him a long time. "Do you believe because you have seen?"

Look up and let your eyes move around the circle of children then back to the picture.

He then slowly looked around the whole circle and said, "Blessed are those who have not seen and yet believe."

When you have enjoyed for a moment the idea that Jesus was present to the disciples in this story of Thomas, put the image down on the underlay.

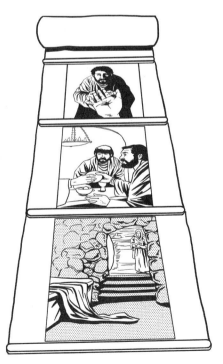

ADDING KNOWN IN DOUBT (VIEW FROM THE CHILDREN'S PERSPECTIVE)

MOVEMENTS

Begin to go around the circle, asking each child if he or she would like to bring something to put by the image on the underlay. Some children may not be able to think of anything or may be too shy to do this, so move on if it looks as if they are stuck. You can come back to them later. If they are still stuck, that is okay.

Many children learn by watching as well as by doing and they may be deeply considering this, despite staying still.

Sometimes children get up, wander for a moment and bring something at random, without knowing why. That's also okay. Be amazed—which is easy— and wonder with them how this is really relevant. Everything in the room is connected in some way, but it is sometimes up to the storyteller to put that into a few words with wonder. Enjoy the items that the children bring to help tell the story.

When you have had time to enjoy the entire layout, invite children, one at a time, to return their chosen materials to the correct shelves.

Then, put the images back on the stand beside you, roll up the underlay, place it back on the stand, and return the lesson to the Pentecost shelf.

When everything is back in its place, you can begin to help children, one at a time, to choose their work.

WORDS

➡ Now I wonder if there is anything in this room that you can bring and put beside this picture to help us tell more about this part of the story? Is there something that just calls to you and seems like it needs to be there? Look around and see.

I will go around the circle and ask each one of you if you would like to go and get something to put beside this image to show more about it.

➡ I don't know what you are going to get.

You are the only one in the world who knows that. If you don't feel like getting something, that's okay. Just enjoy what we make together. You are still part of what we make.

➡ I wonder what you would like to make your work today?

LESSON 10

KNOWING JESUS IN A NEW WAY, PART 4: KNOWN IN THE MORNING

LESSON NOTES

FOCUS: KNOWN IN THE MORNING (JOHN 21:1-23)

● LITURGICAL ACTION
● CORE PRESENTATION

THE MATERIAL

● LOCATION: THE MYSTERY OF PENTECOST SHELF, TOP SHELF—FIRST LESSON
● PIECES: 6 PLAQUES ILLUSTRATED WITH THE RESURRECTION APPEARANCES OF JESUS, 1 PLAQUE ILLUSTRATED WITH THE GIFT OF THE HOLY SPIRIT AT PENTECOST, A STAND TO HOLD THE 7 PLAQUES
● UNDERLAY: 6 WHITE PANELS AND 1 RED PANEL SEPARATED BY NARROW, GOLD PIECES OF WOOD

BACKGROUND

The season of Easter (Eastertide) extends the experience of Easter Sunday for six weeks, but it also helps prepare for the coming of the Mystery of Pentecost. This period is a transition between Jesus' earthly ministry and the coming of the Holy Spirit. It is a time when the disciples and others began to know Jesus in a new way. He is neither simply human nor simply spiritual. He is completely both in a way that is anything but simple.

Jesus' appearances have fascinated people from the disciples, to the opponents of the early Christians, to the present. What did they experience? Clearly it was something very powerful. Paul was an opponent of the Followers of the Way, yet his experience of Jesus after the Resurrection completely changed his life. It turned him around and toward what would later be called "Christian."

Paul provided us with the earliest written list of appearances still available to us. It can be found in what we today call his "first" letter to the church at Corinth (I Corinthians 15:3 – 11). His list began with Cephas, which means "Peter" in Aramaic. It continues with the disciples and then "more than five hundred …most …still alive." James was listed next. He is only the second person Paul specifically named as a participant in this experience in addition to himself, "the least of the apostles." Our task here, however, is not to explain or analyze. It is to tell the story, drawing on the season of Eastertide to guide us by its structure, as we make our way toward Pentecost and the coming of the Holy Spirit in the lives of the disciples and in our own.

This is not to say that the time, place, and identity of those experiencing Jesus in this new way and related matters are not interesting and significant. They are. This is only to say that such talk would shift the emphasis in this introduction from guiding the storytelling to an analysis of the texts and their context, which is a very different kind of communication. Such an analysis can be saved for another time. For now it is enough to say that the scriptural texts each presentation draws on in this series are indicated at the beginning of each lesson.

Our focus here is on Jesus' followers, as they experienced the fearful wonder and astonishment of this transition time. It was a vast adjustment to learn how to know Jesus in this new way. Furthermore, in all of the appearances there is at least an implied call to mission. The disciples were commissioned to spread the good news of the reality they experienced during the transition and in Pentecost. There was no precedent for this. They were called to help God create a new and unknown world! Such a vocation was overwhelming for them, as it is for us today, but we, at least, have this story to guide us. They did not. They had to create God's creation anew, as we must also do in our own time guided by Eastertide and Pentecost.

NOTES ON THE MATERIAL

Everything you need for this presentation is located on the Pentecost Shelf. The rack, sitting on the top shelf, holds both the underlay and the seven images depicting the six appearances and Pentecost. The images stand up in this rack so the children can see the art and be drawn to it.

This presentation is like the "Faces of Easter" although it begins where the "Faces" ends. The underlay is unrolled back toward the storyteller from the middle of the circle rather than away from the storyteller. In the "Faces" the storyteller helps give birth to the narrative of the One who becomes Easter. In this lesson the storyteller is reborn in narrative by the loss, astonishment, and longing of the disciples, as they move inward to receive the Holy Spirit in Pentecost.

This lesson ends like "Faces" with a change of color. The change is from white to red and marks the shift from preparation encounters to the Mystery of Pentecost itself. The moving out in the "Faces of Easter" returns inward with the Pentecost lesson. It marks the new reality that the disciples learned to know and trust. God's elusive presence is not only beyond in the creation and beside us as Jesus, the redemptive companion of the Gospels, but is also within to motivate and sustain us to move on in our journey. The divinity and humanity of Jesus, a coincidence of opposites, is clarified experientially by this process to provide a new way to conceive of what is really good and true and beautiful in life and death.

The rhythm of moving out and within again requires two different kinds of art. In "Faces" the art shows the changing face of the One who is Easter, drawing on the theme of faces in the Old and New Testaments, such as how the face of Moses glowed when he emerged from the Tabernacle. It also draws on the way of saying "intimate presence" in Hebrew with the lovely phrase "face to face." In this series of lessons, however, Jesus' presence is suggested by the faces of the disciples. The children are invited into the perplexity and wonder of the disciples as they see Jesus in this new way. It is the space between them and Jesus that the children are invited to enter, so the centuries can dissolve, enabling the children to be there, as Jesus is here.

SPECIAL NOTES

In conclusion there is an important similarity between this lesson and the "Faces of Easter" that needs special emphasis. At the end of each presentation during the six Sundays of Eastertide the children are invited to choose materials from around the room that will help tell more of the story or that their intuition tells them need to be placed next to each picture, even if they can't articulate why.

For example, when you tell the story of the women at the empty tomb, one child might bring the Mary figure from "The Holy Family" on the altar/focal shelf to put beside the image. Another child might bring the crucifixion marker from "Jesus and Jerusalem" or the whole box of crosses from the enrichment lesson about crosses to put beside the tile. Be open to the surprising connections children make, as they explore the meaning embodied in the stories of the disciples' encounters with the risen Christ. There is much to be learned from them as we make this journey together in Godly Play.

WHERE TO FIND THE MATERIAL

As we have said, the seven parts to the lesson, "Knowing Jesus in a New Way," are found on the top shelf of the Pentecost shelf unit. The classroom map suggests where this might be, but your Godly Play room may not be as fully developed as this one or look exactly like it. You will need to find a way to be creative, following the principles of how the room is laid out. For example, your Godly Play room may not be a perfect rectangle. What do you do then? You do the best you can.

WHERE TO FIND MATERIALS

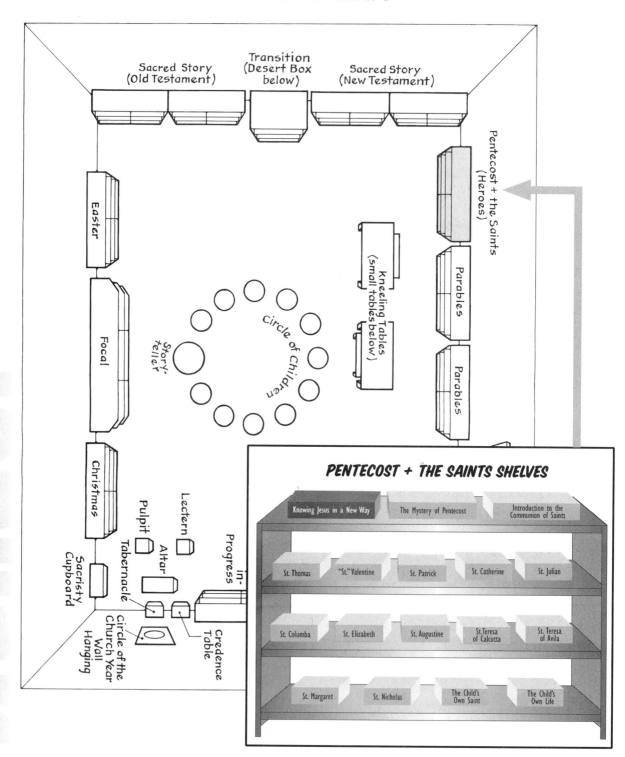

Sacred Story (Old Testament)

Transition (Desert Box below)

Sacred Story (New Testament)

Pentecost + the Saints (Heroes)

Easter

Focal

Christmas

Kneeling Tables (small tables below)

Story-teller

Circle of Children

Parables

Parables

Lectern

Pulpit

Altar

Tabernacle

Sacristy Cupboard

in-Progress

Credence Table

circle of the Church Year Wall Hanging

PENTECOST + THE SAINTS SHELVES

| Knowing Jesus in a New Way | The Mystery of Pentecost | Introduction to the Communion of Saints |

| St. Thomas | "St." Valentine | St. Patrick | St. Catherine | St. Julian |

| St. Columba | St. Elizabeth | St. Augustine | St. Teresa of Calcutta | St. Teresa of Avila |

| St. Margaret | St. Nicholas | The Child's Own Saint | The Child's Own Life |

MOVEMENTS

WORDS

When the children are ready, go and get the material from the shelf. ➡ Watch where I go to get the lesson for today.

Unroll the underlay toward you to the end of the first white section. Summarize the first image (the women at the tomb) while holding it in front of you and then place it on the underlay.

Unroll the underlay to the end of second white section. Summarize the second image (Jesus and two of his followers breaking bread) while holding it in front of you and then place it on the underlay.

Unroll the underlay to the end of the third white section. Summarize the third image (Thomas kneeling before Jesus) while holding it in front of you and then place it on the underlay.

Unroll the underlay to the end of the fourth white section and tell the story while holding the fourth image (the disciples in the boat, fishing in the morning) in front of you. ➡ On the fourth Sunday in the season of Easter we remember how the disciples went north to Galilee, as Jesus told them.

It was a long journey, some eighty miles.

It took about four days to walk.

Many of them were fishermen, so they went to the Sea of Galilee to rest.
This was a place they knew as boys.
They had fished there with their fathers.

Suddenly, Peter stood up and said, "I'm going fishing." The rest went with him to prepare the boat.

Circle the boat in the image with your hand.

Soon they pushed out into the lake and the sail filled with wind.
They fished all night, but they caught nothing. Still, the sounds and smells of the lake comforted them. They were home.

MOVEMENTS	WORDS
Move your finger along the shoreline and point lightly to the figure, fire and smoke in the image. ⟹	In the morning the sky turned pink and then blue. They could make out the shore and someone standing by a fire. They could see the smoke and red glow from the charcoal burning.

"Have you caught anything?"

All they could say was, "No."

"Throw your nets in on the other side."

What could they lose? They pulled in the empty nets and threw them out on the other side. They could feel the fish moving as they held the ropes.

John was not paying attention to fish. He leaned forward and watched the man moving on the shore. He said to Peter, "It is the Lord."

Peter stood up. He jumped. He swam.
He felt the sand under his feet and waded ashore.

The others turned the boat toward land. The nets were so full they could not pull them in, so they dragged them behind the boat.

As they walked toward the fire, the stranger called out, "Bring some fish."

When they gathered around the fire, the stranger was no stranger. They all knew it was Jesus but they were afraid to say anything.

Circle the fire and then...

⟹ "Have some breakfast." There were fish cooking on the fire. He gave them fish and bread. They talked as they ate. The fish and bread also tasted of home.

Then Jesus asked Peter, "Do *you* love me?"
"Yes, of course."
"Feed my lambs."
"Do you *love* me?"
"Yes."
"Tend my sheep."
"Do you love *me*?"

MOVEMENTS	WORDS
	"You already know I do."
	"Feed my sheep."
	He then began to talk to Peter about growing old and how you need help in old age. Sometimes people tell you what to do, even if you don't want them to. Years later they wondered if Jesus had been preparing Peter for his death in Rome as an old man.
	Jesus said, "Follow me."
	Did he mean all of them? No.
...move your finger along the shoreline. ➠	Peter got up and the two of them walked off along the shoreline. Peter looked back and saw John following them. "What about this man? Will he die like the rest of us?"
	"It is not for you to know such things." Peter fell silent and Jesus was gone.
When you have enjoyed for a moment the idea that Jesus was present to the disciples in the morning, put the image down on the underlay, facing the children.	

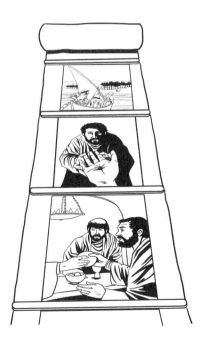

ADDING KNOWN IN THE MORNING (VIEW FROM THE CHILDREN'S PERSPECTIVE)

MOVEMENTS

Begin to go around the circle, asking each child if he or she would like to bring something to put by the image on the underlay. Some children may not be able to think of anything or may be too shy to do this, so move on if it looks as if they are stuck. You can come back to them later. If they are still stuck, that is okay.

Many children learn by watching as well as by doing and they may be deeply considering this, despite staying still.

Sometimes children get up, wander for a moment and bring something at random, without knowing why. That's also okay. Be amazed—which is easy— and wonder with them how this is really relevant. Everything in the room is connected in some way, but it is sometimes up to the storyteller to put that into a few words with wonder. Enjoy the items that the children bring to help tell the story.

When you have had time to enjoy the entire layout, invite children, one at a time, to return their chosen materials to the correct shelves.

Then, put the images back on the stand beside you, roll up the underlay, place it back on the stand, and return the lesson to the Pentecost shelf.

When everything is back in its place, you can begin to help children, one at a time, to choose their work.

WORDS

Now I wonder if there is anything in this room that you can bring and put beside this picture to help us tell more about this part of the story? Is there something that just calls to you and seems like it needs to be there? Look around and see.

I will go around the circle and ask each one of you if you would like to go and get something to put beside this image to show more about it.

I don't know what you are going to get.

You are the only one in the world who knows that. If you don't feel like getting something, that's okay. Just enjoy what we make together. You are still part of what we make.

I wonder what you would like to make your work today?

LESSON 11

KNOWING JESUS IN A NEW WAY, PART 5: KNOWN IN MAKING HIM KNOWN

LESSON NOTES

FOCUS: KNOWN IN MAKING HIM KNOWN (MATTHEW 28: 16-20, MARK 16:15-18)

- LITURGICAL ACTION
- CORE PRESENTATION

THE MATERIAL

- LOCATION: THE MYSTERY OF PENTECOST SHELF, TOP SHELF–FIRST LESSON
- PIECES: 6 PLAQUES ILLUSTRATED WITH THE RESURRECTION APPEARANCES OF JESUS, 1 PLAQUE ILLUSTRATED WITH THE GIFT OF THE HOLY SPIRIT AT PENTECOST, A STAND TO HOLD THE 7 PLAQUES
- UNDERLAY: 6 WHITE PANELS AND 1 RED PANEL SEPARATED BY NARROW, GOLD PIECES OF WOOD

BACKGROUND

The season of Easter (Eastertide) extends the experience of Easter Sunday for six weeks, but it also helps prepare for the coming of the Mystery of Pentecost. This period is a transition between Jesus' earthly ministry and the coming of the Holy Spirit. It is a time when the disciples and others began to know Jesus in a new way. He is neither simply human nor simply spiritual. He is completely both in a way that is anything but simple.

Jesus' appearances have fascinated people from the disciples, to the opponents of the early Christians, to the present. What did they experience? Clearly it was something very powerful. Paul was an opponent of the Followers of the Way, yet his experience of Jesus after the Resurrection completely changed his life. It turned him around and toward what would later be called "Christian."

Paul provided us with the earliest written list of appearances still available to us. It can be found in what we today call his "first" letter to the church at Corinth (I Corinthians 15:3 – 11). His list began with Cephas, which means "Peter" in Aramaic. It continues with the disciples and then "more than five hundred …most …still alive." James was listed next. He is only the second person Paul specifically named as a participant in this experience in addition to himself, "the least of the apostles."

Our task here, however, is not to explain or analyze. It is to tell the story, drawing on the season of Eastertide to guide us by its structure, as we make our way toward Pentecost and the coming of the Holy Spirit in the lives of the disciples and in our own.

This is not to say that the time, place, and identity of those experiencing Jesus in this new way and related matters are not interesting and significant. They are. This is only to say that such talk would shift the emphasis in this introduction from guiding the storytelling to an analysis of the texts and their context, which is a very different kind of communication. Such an analysis can be saved for another time. For now it is enough to say that the scriptural texts each presentation draws on in this series are indicated at the beginning of each lesson.

Our focus here is on Jesus' followers, as they experienced the fearful wonder and astonishment of this transition time. It was a vast adjustment to learn how to know Jesus in this new way. Furthermore, in all of the appearances there is at least an implied call to mission. The disciples were commissioned to spread the good news of the reality they experienced during the transition and in Pentecost. There was no precedent for this. They were called to help God create a new and unknown world! Such a vocation was overwhelming for them, as it is for us today, but we, at least, have this story to guide us. They did not. They had to create God's creation anew, as we must also do in our own time guided by Eastertide and Pentecost.

NOTES ON THE MATERIAL

Everything you need for this presentation is located on the Pentecost Shelf. The rack, sitting on the top shelf, holds both the underlay and the seven images depicting the six appearances and Pentecost. The images stand up in this rack so the children can see the art and be drawn to it.

This presentation is like the "Faces of Easter" although it begins where the "Faces" ends. The underlay is unrolled back toward the storyteller from the middle of the circle rather than away from the storyteller. In the "Faces" the storyteller helps give birth to the narrative of the One who becomes Easter. In this lesson the storyteller is reborn in narrative by the loss, astonishment, and longing of the disciples, as they move inward to receive the Holy Spirit in Pentecost.

This lesson ends like "Faces" with a change of color. The change is from white to red and marks the shift from preparation encounters to the Mystery of Pentecost itself. The moving out in the "Faces of Easter" returns inward with the Pentecost lesson. It marks the new reality that the disciples learned to know and trust. God's elusive presence is not only beyond in the creation and beside us as Jesus, the redemptive companion of the Gospels, but is also within to motivate and sustain us to move on in our journey. The divinity and humanity of Jesus, a coincidence of opposites, is clarified experientially by this process to provide a new way to conceive of what is really good and true and beautiful in life and death.

The rhythm of moving out and within again requires two different kinds of art. In "Faces" the art shows the changing face of the One who is Easter, drawing on the theme of faces in the Old and New Testaments, such as how the face of Moses glowed when he emerged from the Tabernacle. It also draws on the way of saying "intimate presence" in Hebrew with the lovely phrase "face to face." In this series of lessons, however, Jesus' presence is suggested by the faces of the disciples. The children are invited into the perplexity and wonder of the disciples as they see Jesus in this new way. It is the space between them and Jesus that the children are invited to enter, so the centuries can dissolve, enabling the children to be there, as Jesus is here.

SPECIAL NOTES

In conclusion there is an important similarity between this lesson and the "Faces of Easter" that needs special emphasis. At the end of each presentation during the six Sundays of Eastertide the children are invited to choose materials from around the room that will help tell more of the story or that their intuition tells them need to be placed next to each picture, even if they can't articulate why.

For example, when you tell the story of the women at the empty tomb, one child might bring the Mary figure from "The Holy Family" on the altar/focal shelf to put beside the image. Another child might bring the crucifixion marker from "Jesus and Jerusalem" or the whole box of crosses from the enrichment lesson about crosses to put beside the tile. Be open to the surprising connections children make, as they explore the meaning embodied in the stories of the disciples' encounters with the risen Christ. There is much to be learned from them as we make this journey together in Godly Play.

WHERE TO FIND THE MATERIAL

As we have said, the seven parts to the lesson "Knowing Jesus in a New Way" are found on the top shelf of the Pentecost shelf unit. The classroom map suggests where this might be, but your Godly Play room may not be as fully developed as this one or look exactly like it. You will need to find a way to be creative, following the principles of how the room is laid out. For example, your Godly Play room may not be a perfect rectangle. What do you do then? You do the best you can.

WHERE TO FIND MATERIALS

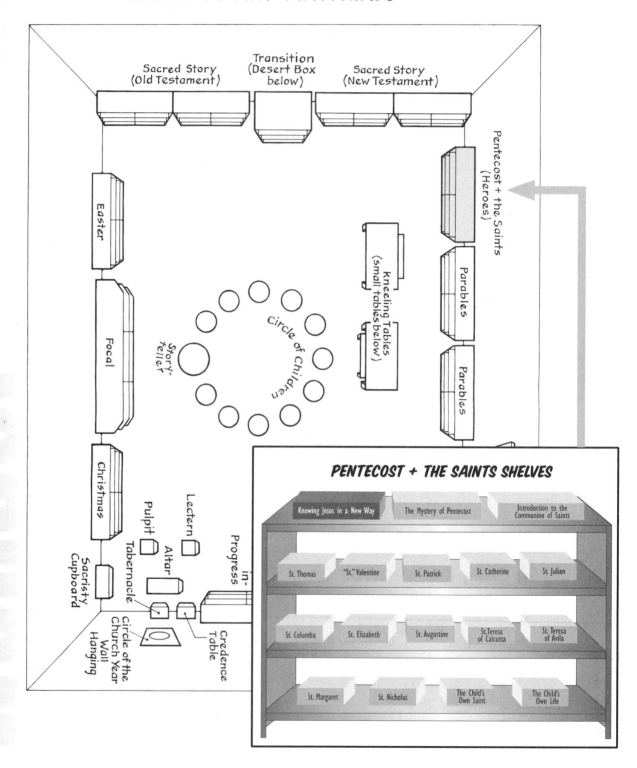

Sacred Story (Old Testament)

Transition (Desert Box below)

Sacred Story (New Testament)

Pentecost + the Saints (Heroes)

Easter

Focal

Christmas

Kneeling Tables (small tables below)

Parables

Parables

Story-teller

Circle of Children

Sacristy Cupboard

Tabernacle

Altar

Pulpit

Lectern

In-Progress

Circle of the Church Year Wall Hanging

Credence Table

PENTECOST + THE SAINTS SHELVES

Knowing Jesus in a New Way | The Mystery of Pentecost | Introduction to the Communion of Saints

St. Thomas | "St." Valentine | St. Patrick | St. Catherine | St. Julian

St. Columba | St. Elizabeth | St. Augustine | St. Teresa of Calcutta | St. Teresa of Avila

St. Margaret | St. Nicholas | The Child's Own Saint | The Child's Own Life

MOVEMENTS	WORDS
When the children are ready, go and get the material from the shelf. ➠	Watch where I go to get the lesson for today.
Unroll the underlay toward you to the end of the first white section. Summarize the first image (the women at the tomb) while holding it in front of you and then place it on the underlay.	
Unroll the underlay to the end of second white section. Summarize the second image (Jesus and two of his followers breaking bread) while holding it in front of you and then place it on the underlay.	
Unroll the underlay to the end of the third white section. Summarize the third image (Thomas kneeling before Jesus) while holding it in front of you and then place it on the underlay.	
Unroll the underlay to the end of the fourth white section. Summarize the fourth image (the disciples in the boat, fishing in the morning) while holding it in front of you and then place it on the underlay.	
Unroll the underlay to the end of the fifth white section and tell the story while holding the fifth image (Jesus speaking to the disciples) in front of you. ➠	On the fifth Sunday in the season of Easter we remember how all the disciples gathered in Galilee. They gathered together and went to the mountain to meet Jesus. He was already there. It was good to see him, even in this new way, but what were they supposed to do now?
Move your hand around the faces of the disciples listening. ➠	Listen. He was talking again. What was that? "All authority in heaven and on earth has been given to me."
Point to and then move your hand lightly up and down the figure of Jesus. ➠	What was he talking about? Then he said something that they could understand, but did not want to hear.

MOVEMENTS

WORDS

Move your hand across the curve of ➧ *Jesus' outstretched arms and into the mountains and sky beyond them.*

"Go everywhere. Tell my story, even this part, to everyone. Show them how to be good disciples. Tell them the story so they can become part of it. Baptize them in the name of the Father, and of the Son and of the Holy Spirit."

This was too far to travel, too much to do. Then in their dismay they heard him say, "I am with you *always* to the end of the age." Then he was gone.

What did he mean?

As they walked back south to Jerusalem, they knew they had been followers, now they were to be leaders.
They had been sheep, now they were to be shepherds.
They had come home for the last time, now they were to make a home for others.

When you have felt for a moment the presence of Jesus to the disciples as he sent them out to share their story, place the image on the underlay.

ADDING KNOWN IN MAKING HIM KNOWN (VIEW FROM THE CHILDREN'S PERSPECTIVE)

MOVEMENTS

Begin to go around the circle, asking each child if he or she would like to bring something to put by the image on the underlay. Some children may not be able to think of anything or may be too shy to do this, so move on if it looks as if they are stuck. You can come back to them later. If they are still stuck, that is okay.

Many children learn by watching as well as by doing and they may be deeply considering this, despite staying still.

Sometimes children get up, wander for a moment and bring something at random, without knowing why. That's also okay. Be amazed—which is easy—and wonder with them how this is really relevant. Everything in the room is connected in some way, but it is sometimes up to the storyteller to put that into a few words with wonder. Enjoy the items that the children bring to help tell the story.

When you have had time to enjoy the entire layout, invite children, one at a time, to return their chosen materials to the correct shelves.

Then, put the images back on the stand beside you, roll up the underlay, place it back on the stand, and return the lesson to the Pentecost shelf.

When everything is back in its place, you can begin to help children, one at a time, to choose their work.

WORDS

Now I wonder if there is anything in this room that you can bring and put beside this picture to help us tell more about this part of the story? Is there something that just calls to you and seems like it needs to be there? Look around and see.

I will go around the circle and ask each one of you if you would like to go and get something to put beside this image to show more about it.

I don't know what you are going to get. You are the only one in the world who knows that. If you don't feel like getting something, that's okay. Just enjoy what we make together. You are still part of what we make.

I wonder what you would like to make your work today?

LESSON 12

KNOWING JESUS IN A NEW WAY, PART 6: KNOWN IN WAITING

LESSON NOTES

FOCUS: KNOWN IN WAITING (MARK 16:19-20, LUKE 24:50-53, ACTS 1:9-12)

- ● LITURGICAL ACTION
- ● CORE PRESENTATION

THE MATERIAL

- ● LOCATION: THE MYSTERY OF PENTECOST SHELF, TOP SHELF—FIRST LESSON
- ● PIECES: 6 PLAQUES ILLUSTRATED WITH THE RESURRECTION APPEARANCES OF JESUS, 1 PLAQUE ILLUSTRATED WITH THE GIFT OF THE HOLY SPIRIT AT PENTECOST, A STAND TO HOLD THE 7 PLAQUES
- ● UNDERLAY: 6 WHITE PANELS AND 1 RED PANEL SEPARATED BY NARROW, GOLD PIECES OF WOOD

BACKGROUND

The season of Easter (Eastertide) extends the experience of Easter Sunday for six weeks, but it also helps prepare for the coming of the Mystery of Pentecost. This period is a transition between Jesus' earthly ministry and the coming of the Holy Spirit. It is a time when the disciples and others began to know Jesus in a new way. He is neither simply human nor simply spiritual. He is completely both in a way that is anything but simple.

Jesus' appearances have fascinated people from the disciples, to the opponents of the early Christians, to the present. What did they experience? Clearly it was something very powerful. Paul was an opponent of the Followers of the Way, yet his experience of Jesus after the Resurrection completely changed his life. It turned him around and toward what would later be called "Christian."

Paul provided us with the earliest written list of appearances still available to us. It can be found in what we today call his "first" letter to the church at Corinth (I Corinthians 15:3 – 11). His list began with Cephas, which means "Peter" in Aramaic. It continues with the disciples and then "more than five hundred …most …still alive." James was listed next. He is only the second person Paul specifically named as a participant in this experience in addition to himself, "the least of the apostles." Our task here, however, is not to explain or analyze. It is to tell the story, drawing on the season of Eastertide to guide us by its structure, as we make our way toward Pentecost and the coming of the Holy Spirit in the lives of the disciples and in our own.

This is not to say that the time, place, and identity of those experiencing Jesus in this new way and related matters are not interesting and significant. They are. This is only to say that such talk would shift the emphasis in this introduction from guiding the storytelling to an analysis of the texts and their context, which is a very different kind of communication. Such an analysis can be saved for another time. For now it is enough to say that the scriptural texts each presentation draws on in this series are indicated at the beginning of each lesson.

Our focus here is on Jesus' followers, as they experienced the fearful wonder and astonishment of this transition time. It was a vast adjustment to learn how to know Jesus in this new way. Furthermore, in all of the appearances there is at least an implied call to mission. The disciples were commissioned to spread the good news of the reality they experienced during the transition and in Pentecost. There was no precedent for this. They were called to help God create a new and unknown world! Such a vocation was overwhelming for them, as it is for us today, but we, at least, have this story to guide us. They did not. They had to create God's creation anew, as we must also do in our own time guided by Eastertide and Pentecost.

NOTES ON THE MATERIAL

Everything you need for this presentation is located on the Pentecost Shelf. The rack, sitting on the top shelf, holds both the underlay and the seven images depicting the six appearances and Pentecost. The images stand up in this rack so the children can see the art and be drawn to it.

This presentation is like the "Faces of Easter" although it begins where the "Faces" ends. The underlay is unrolled back toward the storyteller from the middle of the circle rather than away from the storyteller. In the "Faces" the storyteller helps give birth to the narrative of the One who becomes Easter. In this lesson the storyteller is reborn in narrative by the loss, astonishment, and longing of the disciples, as they move inward to receive the Holy Spirit in Pentecost.

This lesson ends like "Faces" with a change of color. The change is from white to red and marks the shift from preparation encounters to the Mystery of Pentecost itself. The moving out in the "Faces of Easter" returns inward with the Pentecost lesson. It marks the new reality that the disciples learned to know and trust. God's elusive presence is not only beyond in the creation and beside us as Jesus, the redemptive companion of the Gospels, but is also within to motivate and sustain us to move on in our journey. The divinity and humanity of Jesus, a coincidence of opposites, is clarified experientially by this process to provide a new way to conceive of what is really good and true and beautiful in life and death.

The rhythm of moving out and within again requires two different kinds of art. In "Faces" the art shows the changing face of the One who is Easter, drawing on the theme of faces in the Old and New Testaments, such as how the face of Moses glowed when he emerged from the Tabernacle. It also draws on the way of saying "intimate presence" in Hebrew with the lovely phrase "face to face." In this series of lessons, however, Jesus' presence is suggested by the faces of the disciples. The children are invited into the perplexity and wonder of the disciples as they see Jesus in this new way. It is the space between them and Jesus that the children are invited to enter, so the centuries can dissolve, enabling the children to be there, as Jesus is here.

SPECIAL NOTES

In conclusion there is an important similarity between this lesson and the "Faces of Easter" that needs special emphasis. At the end of each presentation during the six Sundays of Eastertide the children are invited to choose materials from around the room that will help tell more of the story or that their intuition tells them need to be placed next to each picture, even if they can't articulate why.

For example, when you tell the story of the women at the empty tomb, one child might bring the Mary figure from "The Holy Family" on the altar/focal shelf to put beside the image. Another child might bring the crucifixion marker from "Jesus and Jerusalem" or the whole box of crosses from the enrichment lesson about crosses to put beside the tile. Be open to the surprising connections children make, as they explore the meaning embodied in the stories of the disciples' encounters with the risen Christ. There is much to be learned from them as we make this journey together in Godly Play.

WHERE TO FIND THE MATERIAL

As we have said, the seven parts to the lesson "Knowing Jesus in a New Way" are found on the top shelf of the Pentecost shelf unit. The classroom map suggests where this might be, but your Godly Play room may not be as fully developed as this one or look exactly like it. You will need to find a way to be creative, following the principles of how the room is laid out. For example, your Godly Play room may not be a perfect rectangle. What do you do then? You do the best you can.

WHERE TO FIND MATERIALS

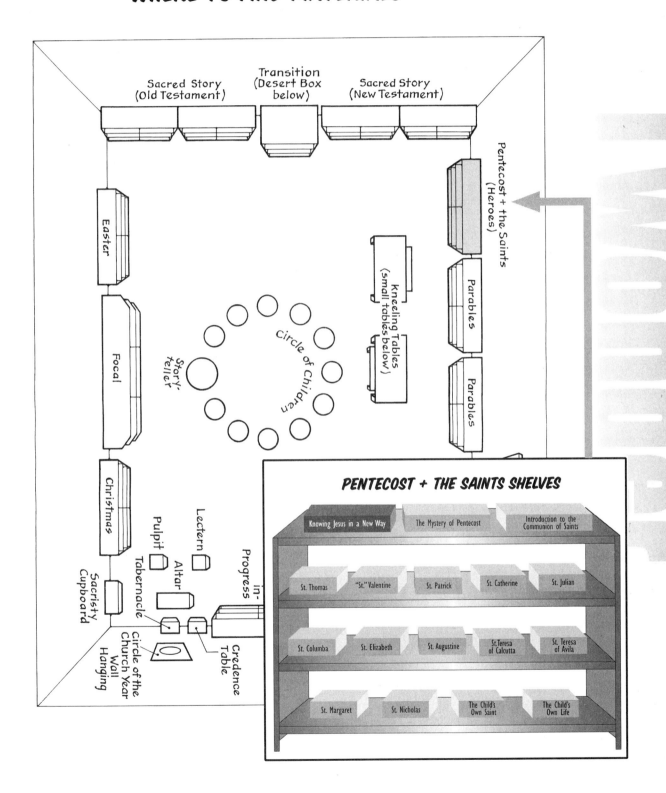

PLAY

I wonder

PENTECOST + THE SAINTS SHELVES

MOVEMENTS	**WORDS**

When the children are ready, go and get the material from the shelf. ➠ Watch where I go to get the lesson for today.

Unroll the underlay toward you to the end of the first white section. Summarize the first image (the women at the tomb) while holding it in front of you and then place it on the underlay.

Unroll the underlay to the end of second white section. Summarize the second image (Jesus and two of his disciples breaking bread) while holding it in front of you and then place it on the underlay.

Unroll the underlay to the end of the third white section. Summarize the third image (Thomas kneeling before Jesus) while holding it in front of you and then place it on the underlay.

Unroll the underlay to the end of the fourth white section. Summarize the fourth image (the disciples in the boat, fishing in the morning) while holding it in front of you and then place it on the underlay.

Unroll the underlay to the end of the fifth white section. Summarize the fifth image (Jesus speaking to the disciples) while holding it in front of you and then place it on the underlay.

Unroll the underlay to end of the sixth white section and tell the story while holding the sixth image (the Ascension) in front of you. ➠ On the sixth Sunday in the season of Easter we remember how the disciples returned to Jerusalem. They gathered again in their room and Jesus was there.

They were more comfortable now with the new way of knowing Him, so they asked many questions, most of them were foolish.

"Lord, will you restore the kingdom to Israel?"

MOVEMENTS	WORDS
	Jesus cut short such talk. "It is not for you to know the times or seasons."
	He then led them out of the room and through the streets. They went beyond the walls of Jerusalem to a hillside, perhaps near Bethany.
Move your finger around the figures in a circle. ⬛▶	Jesus stopped and they gathered around him. He lifted up his hands, looking at each one, and blessed them. He then "withdrew" and "a cloud took him out of sight."
Now move your finger around each face looking up. ⬛▶	The disciples stood looking into the sky until someone said, "Why are you looking up into the sky?" There were two men standing there, dressed in white. The disciples felt silly. What *were* they doing looking up into the sky for what they could no longer see? The strangers then answered their own question. "This was Jesus. He is gone now, as you have known him." It seemed like a great weight was lifted from their shoulders.
	The disciples turned and walked back to Jerusalem. Now they had to wait. What was this Holy Spirit he said was coming? How would they know it when it arrived? They waited and waited.
	While they waited they found someone to replace Judas. God helped them choose Matthias, so now they were The Twelve, once more, but they still had to keep waiting. How long would it take for the Holy Spirit to come?
When you have enjoyed for a moment the idea that Jesus was present to the disciples as they watched him ascend and that the disciples then went back to Jerusalem to wait, place the image on the underlay.	

MOVEMENTS

WORDS

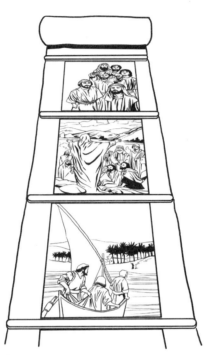

ADDING KNOWN IN WAITING (VIEW FROM THE CHILDREN'S PERSPECTIVE)

Begin to go around the circle, asking each child if he or she would like to bring something to put by the image on the underlay. Some children may not be able to think of anything or may be too shy to do this, so move on if it looks as if they are stuck. You can come back to them later. If they are still stuck, that is okay.

➧ Now I wonder if there is anything in this room that you can bring and put beside this picture to help us tell more about this part of the story? Is there something that just calls to you and seems like it needs to be there? Look around and see.

I will go around the circle and ask each one of you if you would like to go and get something to put beside this image to show more about it.

Many children learn by watching as well as by doing and they may be deeply considering this, despite staying still.

Sometimes children get up, wander for a moment and bring something at random, without knowing why. That's also okay. Be amazed—which is easy—and wonder with them how this is really relevant. Everything in the room is connected in some way, but it is sometimes up to the storyteller to put that into a few words with wonder. Enjoy the items that the children bring to help tell the story.

➧ I don't know what you are going to get. You are the only one in the world who knows that. If you don't feel like getting something, that's okay. Just enjoy what we make together. You are still part of what we make.

MOVEMENTS

When you have had time to enjoy the entire layout, invite children, one at a time, to return their chosen materials to the correct shelves.

Then, put the images back on the stand beside you, roll up the underlay, place it back on the stand, and return the lesson to the Pentecost shelf.

When everything is back in its place, you can begin to help children, one at a time, to choose their work.

WORDS

I wonder what you would like to make your work today?

LESSON 13

KNOWING JESUS IN A NEW WAY, PART 7: KNOWN BY THE HOLY SPIRIT

LESSON NOTES

FOCUS: KNOWN BY THE HOLY SPIRIT (ACTS 2:1-13)

● LITURGICAL ACTION

● CORE PRESENTATION

THE MATERIAL

● LOCATION: THE MYSTERY OF PENTECOST SHELF, TOP SHELF–FIRST LESSON

● PIECES: 6 PLAQUES ILLUSTRATED WITH THE RESURRECTION APPEARANCES OF JESUS, 1 PLAQUE ILLUSTRATED WITH THE GIFT OF THE HOLY SPIRIT AT PENTECOST, A STAND TO HOLD THE 7 PLAQUES

● UNDERLAY: 6 WHITE PANELS AND 1 RED PANEL SEPARATED BY NARROW, GOLD PIECES OF WOOD

BACKGROUND

The season of Easter (Eastertide) extends the experience of Easter Sunday for six weeks, but it also helps prepare for the coming of the Mystery of Pentecost. This period is a transition between Jesus' earthly ministry and the coming of the Holy Spirit. It is a time when the disciples and others began to know Jesus in a new way. He is neither simply human nor simply spiritual. He is completely both in a way that is anything but simple.

Jesus' appearances have fascinated people from the disciples, to the opponents of the early Christians, to the present. What did they experience? Clearly it was something very powerful. Paul was an opponent of the Followers of the Way, yet his experience of Jesus after the Resurrection completely changed his life. It turned him around and toward what would later be called "Christian."

Paul provided us with the earliest written list of appearances still available to us. It can be found in what we today call his "first" letter to the church at Corinth (I Corinthians 15:3 – 11). His list began with Cephas, which means "Peter" in Aramaic. It continues with the disciples and then "more than five hundred …most …still alive." James was listed next. He is only the second person Paul specifically named as a participant in this experience in addition to himself, "the least of the apostles." Our task here, however, is not to explain or analyze. It is to tell the story, drawing on the season of

Eastertide to guide us by its structure, as we make our way toward Pentecost and the coming of the Holy Spirit in the lives of the disciples and in our own.

This is not to say that the time, place, and identity of those experiencing Jesus in this new way and related matters are not interesting and significant. They are. This is only to say that such talk would shift the emphasis in this introduction from guiding the storytelling to an analysis of the texts and their context, which is a very different kind of communication. Such an analysis can be saved for another time. For now it is enough to say that the scriptural texts each presentation draws on in this series are indicated at the beginning of each lesson.

Our focus here is on Jesus' followers, as they experienced the fearful wonder and astonishment of this transition time. It was a vast adjustment to learn how to know Jesus in this new way. Furthermore, in all of the appearances there is at least an implied call to mission. The disciples were commissioned to spread the good news of the reality they experienced during the transition and in Pentecost. There was no precedent for this. They were called to help God create a new and unknown world! Such a vocation was overwhelming for them, as it is for us today, but we, at least, have this story to guide us. They did not. They had to create God's creation anew, as we must also do in our own time guided by Eastertide and Pentecost.

NOTES ON THE MATERIAL

Everything you need for this presentation is located on the Pentecost Shelf. The rack, sitting on the top shelf, holds both the underlay and the seven images depicting the six appearances and Pentecost. The images stand up in this rack so the children can see the art and be drawn to it.

This presentation is like the "Faces of Easter" although it begins where the "Faces" ends. The underlay is unrolled back toward the storyteller from the middle of the circle rather than away from the storyteller. In the "Faces" the storyteller helps give birth to the narrative of the One who becomes Easter. In this lesson the storyteller is reborn in narrative by the loss, astonishment, and longing of the disciples, as they move inward to receive the Holy Spirit in Pentecost.

This lesson ends like "Faces" with a change of color. The change is from white to red and marks the shift from preparation encounters to the Mystery of Pentecost itself. The moving out in the "Faces of Easter" returns inward with the Pentecost lesson. It marks the new reality that the disciples learned to know and trust. God's elusive presence is not only beyond in the creation and beside us as Jesus, the redemptive companion of the Gospels, but is also within to motivate and sustain us to move on in our journey. The divinity and humanity of Jesus, a coincidence of opposites, is clarified experientially by this process to provide a new way to conceive of what is really good and true and beautiful in life and death.

The rhythm of moving out and within again requires two different kinds of art. In "Faces" the art shows the changing face of the One who is Easter, drawing on the theme of faces in the Old and New Testaments, such as how the face of Moses glowed when he emerged from the Tabernacle. It also draws on the way of saying "intimate presence" in Hebrew with the lovely phrase "face to face." In this series of lessons, however, Jesus' presence is suggested by the faces of the disciples. The children are invited into the perplexity and wonder of the disciples as they see Jesus in this new way. It is the space between them and Jesus that the children are invited to enter, so the centuries can dissolve, enabling the children to be there, as Jesus is here.

SPECIAL NOTES

In conclusion there is an important similarity between this lesson and the "Faces of Easter" that needs special emphasis. At the end of each presentation during the six Sundays of Eastertide the children are invited to choose materials from around the room that will help tell more of the story or that their intuition tells them need to be placed next to each picture, even if they can't articulate why.

For example, when you tell the story of the women at the empty tomb, one child might bring the Mary figure from "The Holy Family" on the altar/focal shelf to put beside the image. Another child might bring the crucifixion marker from "Jesus and Jerusalem" or the whole box of crosses from the enrichment lesson about crosses to put beside the tile. Be open to the surprising connections children make, as they explore the meaning embodied in the stories of the disciples' encounters with the risen Christ. There is much to be learned from them as we make this journey together in Godly Play.

WHERE TO FIND THE MATERIAL

As we have said, the seven parts to the lesson "Knowing Jesus in a New Way" are found on the top shelf of the Pentecost shelf unit. The classroom map suggests where this might be, but your Godly Play room may not be as fully developed as this one or look exactly like it. You will need to find a way to be creative, following the principles of how the room is laid out. For example, your Godly Play room may not be a perfect rectangle. What do you do then? You do the best you can.

WHERE TO FIND MATERIALS

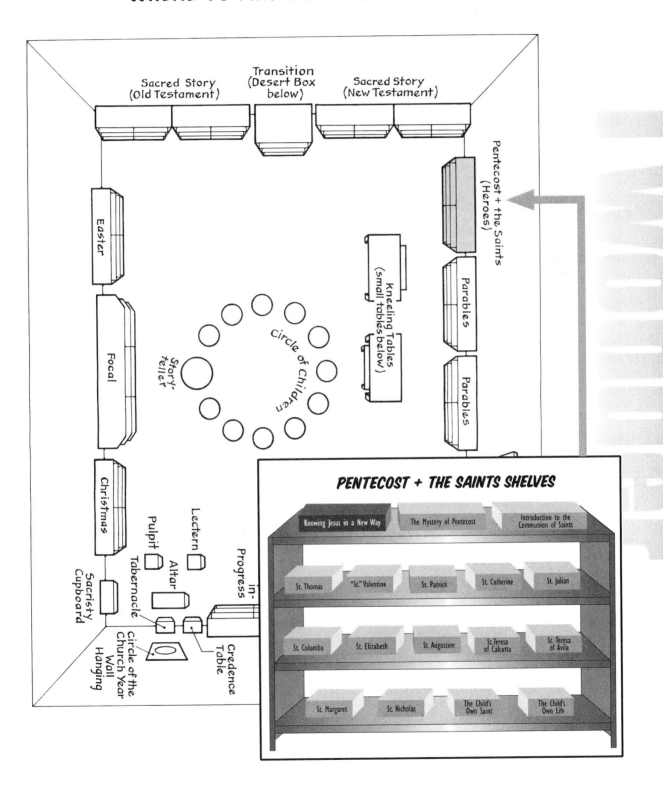

PENTECOST + THE SAINTS SHELVES

Knowing Jesus in a New Way | The Mystery of Pentecost | Introduction to the Communion of Saints

St. Thomas | "St." Valentine | St. Patrick | St. Catherine | St. Julian

St. Columba | St. Elizabeth | St. Augustine | St. Teresa of Calcutta | St. Teresa of Avila

St. Margaret | St. Nicholas | The Child's Own Saint | The Child's Own Life

MOVEMENTS

WORDS

When the children are ready, go and get ➡ the material from the shelf.

Watch where I go to get the lesson for today.

Unroll the underlay toward you to the end of the first white section. Summarize the first image (the women at the tomb) while holding it in front of you and then place it on the underlay.

Unroll the underlay to the end of second white section. Summarize the second image (Jesus and two of his disciples breaking bread) while holding it in front of you and then place it on the underlay.

Unroll the underlay to the end of the third white section. Summarize the third image (Thomas kneeling before Jesus) while holding it in front of you and then place it on the underlay.

Unroll the underlay to the end of the fourth white section. Summarize the fourth image (the disciples in the boat, fishing in the morning) while holding it in front of you and then place it on the underlay.

Unroll the underlay to the end of the fifth white section. Summarize the fifth image (Jesus speaking to the disciples) while holding it in front of you and then place it on the underlay.

Unroll the underlay to end of the sixth white section. Summarize the sixth image (the Ascension) while holding it in front of you.

MOVEMENTS

Leave the red part of the underlay rolled ⇒
so the children cannot see it and tell the
last part of the story (the coming of the
Holy Spirit) while holding the image in
front of you.

WORDS

Finally, it was the day of Pentecost or *Shavuot (Sha-voo-ot),* as it is known in Hebrew.

It was a time of greening and blooming in the spring. The grain was ripe in the fields. The streets of Jerusalem were full of Jews from all over the Roman Empire going to the Temple to remember the legendary fifty days between the Passover and when God gave Moses the Ten Commandments at Mount Sinai.

The disciples remained in their room, a place some say was the very room where they shared the Last Supper with Jesus. They talked quietly and prayed.

Suddenly, they heard the sound of a mighty wind. It filled the whole house. Bits of fire began to dance around each one. The Holy Spirit had come. Even their tongues felt on fire. In their joy they rushed out into the streets to tell everyone!

The people passing by on the way to the Temple thought they were crazy. Maybe they had drunk too much wine. Still, what they said was understood by all—no matter what language they spoke.

Peter stepped into this chaos with a confidence and calm that the disciples had never seen before. "These people are not drunk, like you think. After all, it is only morning. What has happened is what the prophet Joel wrote about. He said that God will pour out God's spirit on us so that our sons and daughters will prophesy, the young will see visions, and the old will dream dreams. This is what just happened!"

Many passed on by to keep their great traditions and live good lives. Others listened and became baptized.

So, this is why the color of Pentecost is red. It is the color of great joy and of fire.

As you mention the color of Pentecost,
unroll the underlay all the way, revealing
the red section.

MOVEMENTS

WORDS

Somewhere the dove that had descended from the heavens at Jesus' baptism must have been smiling to see all of this. What was happening was like a baptism, but not one with water.

This was a baptism with fire.

Amen.

When you have enjoyed for a moment the idea of being filled with the Holy Spirit and rushing to the street to tell others about it, place this image on the red section of the underlay.

ADDING KNOWN BY THE HOLY SPIRIT (VIEW FROM THE CHILDREN'S PERSPECTIVE)

Begin to go around the circle, asking each child if he or she would like to bring something to put by the image on the underlay. Some children may not be able to think of anything or may be too shy to do this, so move on if it looks as if they are stuck. You can come back to them later. If they are still stuck, that is okay.

Now I wonder if there is anything in this room that you can bring and put beside this picture to help us tell more about this part of the story? Is there something that just calls to you and seems like it needs to be there? Look around and see.

I will go around the circle and ask each one of you if you would like to go and get something to put beside this image to show more about it.

MOVEMENTS

Many children learn by watching as well as by doing and they may be deeply considering this, despite staying still.

Sometimes children get up, wander for a moment and bring something at random, without knowing why. That's also okay. Be amazed—which is easy— and wonder with them how this is really relevant. Everything in the room is connected in some way, but it is sometimes up to the storyteller to put that into a few words with wonder. Enjoy the items that the children bring to help tell the story.

When you have had time to enjoy the entire layout, invite children, one at a time, to return their chosen materials to the correct shelves.

Then, put the images back on the stand beside you, roll up the underlay, place it back on the stand, and return the lesson to the Pentecost shelf.

When everything is back in its place, you can begin to help children, one at a time, to choose their work.

WORDS

I don't know what you are going to get.

You are the only one in the world who knows that. If you don't feel like getting something, that's okay. Just enjoy what we make together. You are still part of what we make.

I wonder what you would like to make your work today?

LESSON 14

THE CHURCH

LESSON NOTES

FOCUS: CHURCH SPACE AND INNER SPACE

● AN "AFTERWARDS" LESSON, ONE OF THE LESSONS ABOUT WHAT HAS TAKEN PLACE IN THE CHURCH SINCE THE TIME OF THE SCRIPTURES

THE MATERIAL

● LOCATION: IN A DEVELOPED CLASSROOM THIS LESSON SITS ON ITS OWN SHELF BETWEEN THE PENTECOST SHELF AND THE COMMUNION OF SAINTS SHELF. THE MATERIAL ITSELF SITS ON THE TOP SHELF WITH A BASKET FOR PARTS OF THE CHURCH MODEL BELOW. IN ADDITION THE LOWER SHELVES HOLD PICTURES OF VARIOUS KINDS OF CHURCHES, BOOKS ABOUT STAINED GLASS WINDOWS, THE BUILDING OF CATHEDRALS, AND OTHER RELATED SUPPORTING MATERIALS.

● PIECES: THE MATERIAL SITS ON A BASE AND INCLUDES PIECES THAT FORM FIVE SHAPES FOR THE CHURCH. A SMALL TABLE TO REPRESENT AN ALTAR (TABLE), WHICH IS MOVED WITHIN THE CHURCH SPACE AND REMOVED AT THE END OF THE DECONSTRUCTION BEFORE REPLACING THE TABLE AND REBUILDING THE CHURCH MODEL.

BACKGROUND

Jesus did not say much if anything directly about the church that was born at Pentecost in a simple room in Jerusalem about 33 AD. The word "church" (*ekklesia* in Greek) is used only twice in the four Gospels, which are, of course, written in Greek. The first use was in Matthew 16:18, referring to the "church" being built on Peter, the rock. The second use was also in Matthew at 18:17 and refers to a situation when someone sins against you. You are to confront them in private, but if they won't listen in private, you are to tell it to *the church*. If that does no good, then ignore the person's actions. Jesus did communicate, however, by word and deed about the established religion of his day, which was focused on the Temple in Jerusalem. So, by implication we can surmise what Jesus might say about the established church of our time.

When the New Testament is considered as a whole the word *church* is used some 115 times, mostly in Acts and the letters. On at least 92 occasions these are references to a local congregation. The rest of the time the word is used to refer to the church in general. For example, references to the general church may be found in Ephesians, calling it the household of God with Christ as the cornerstone (2.20). This letter has something to say about the church in nearly every chapter.

The most famous and dynamic metaphor for *the church* is that it embodies Christ. This "body" lives in a way which expresses unity and diversity—as described in Romans 12, 1 Corinthians 12, and in Ephesians (1:22-23; 2:19-22; 4:15-16). The core metaphor for this lesson is about how the many dimensions of Christ's "body" can be found in various shapes of churches, which can be internalized by those who gather there to shape their spirituality, as the search for the elusive presence of God continues beyond Scripture. This core metaphor is especially evoked by the wondering question: "Now, what do we really need to have, to have a church?"

The early Christians met mostly in homes (Acts 5:42), probably around the table. They met the day after the Sabbath, on the first day of the week, in recognition of Christ's resurrection on a Sunday. In I Corinthians 16:2 we read that on the first day of the week Christians were to put something aside for the needy. They also prayed (Acts 12:12), read scripture (James 1:22), broke bread, and shared the cup (I Corinthians 11:20-29). Acts 2:42 says, "They devoted themselves to the apostles teaching and fellowship, the breaking of bread and the prayers."

In this lesson the People of God continue following God's elusive presence, hidden and yet revealed. In the past God's presence was mediated by the Tabernacle and then the Temple. It was then mediated for Christians by the Risen Lord, who *is* the church when it *is* the church. After the Romans destroyed the Temple and the city of Jerusalem in 70CE there was no choice but to meet in homes, as the Jews and Christians did. The Jews also began to build synagogues for community worship, even in Jerusalem where they were no longer welcome, and the Christians began to develop their own places for community worship as well.

God's presence is not contained in a place. It may be found in any place, and among the people who gather in God's name. What a church building provides is a powerful symbol of Christ's indwelling presence to support and guide our inner life and to give shape and identity to our common lives. Sometimes, however, churches can be something larger.

Pierre Teilhard de Chardin S.J.—the theologian, philosopher, paleontologist, and geologist—spent many years in the Gobi Desert studying the origins of the earth and human beings. He was instrumental in the discovery of both the Piltdown Man and the Peking Man. He once wrote in this geographical and intellectual vastness, "Since, Lord, once again…in the steppes of Asia, I have neither bread nor wine nor altar, I will raise myself above these symbols up to the pure majesty of Reality and I, your priest, will offer You upon the altar of the Whole Earth, the labour and the suffering of the world." (Quoted in Robert Maguire and Keith Murray, *Modern Churches of the World*, 8). The church, then, might be the whole universe. The altar within it becomes "the altar of the Whole Earth." Teilhard de Chardin also wrote about the universe as a "living host," the bread of Holy Communion. Much closer to home, we might also find such vastness and symbolic richness in the circle of children we serve.

This brings us back to Solomon's question, which was included in "The Ark and the Temple" in *Volume 2*. At the dedication of the first Temple he stood before the altar and spread forth his hands in prayer. "But will God dwell indeed with man on the earth? Behold, heaven and the highest heaven cannot contain thee; how much less this house which I have built. Yet have regard to the prayer of thy servant and to his supplication, O Lord my God…" (2 Chronicles 6:18–20). Solomon's question is always *the* question about churches and the shape of our encounter with the living God. The answer to Solomon's question is "Yes" and "No." *Deus absconditus atque praesens.* God is hidden and yet present. Even in God's apparent absence, God is there, playing hide and seek with us, where the goal of the game is for *it to continue*, not for God to be so well found or so well hidden that the game is over.

Samuel Terrien has observed in his book *The Elusive Presence* (1978) that when God's presence is guaranteed, as by the clergy in a particular building, it is no longer a living presence. God's presence cannot be domesticated. The way he put this was to say: "The proprietary sight of the glory destroys the vision, whether in the temple of Zion or in the Eucharistic body. ... In biblical faith presence eludes but does not delude (476)." This is why the church remains a holy place in absence as well as presence, sometimes an aid and sometimes a distraction, as we move forward with the God who is beyond in creation, beside us as Jesus our redemptive companion, and within as the Holy Spirit.

During the presentation the model is taken apart step-by-step to suggest the church's many forms and the continuing search for the One who is both hidden and revealed within its walls. Once the model is deconstructed to its base showing the destruction of the Temple, it is then built back so that the wondering question that follows King Solomon's prayer can be asked: "Now, what do we really need to have, to have a church?"

NOTES ON THE MATERIAL

The material is a model of a church sitting on a large, wooden base. As it is taken apart, other shapes for churches are found, roughly tracing the story of church shapes and theology back to the 1st century. When the lesson continues the model is rebuilt in the opposite order to return to the present. As the model is taken apart, the removed pieces are placed on either side of the storyteller. Here are the pieces in order of their removal:

1. The towers.
2. The high walls and their supporting structures (the flying buttresses)
3. The transepts (the arms of the cross-shaped space)
4. The basilica (the curved end, called the apse, and the rectangular walls)
5. The round church
6. The table
7. The empty base evokes the desolation when the first Christians and the Jews sought God's elusive presence after the destruction of the Temple and the city of Jerusalem

As the model is put back together from the base (#7), the story of the various shapes of churches is expanded, leading to wondering at the end, after the towers are replaced (#1), about what we really need to have to make a church. The variety of shapes also suggests changes in the theology and spirituality of the church. The placement of the altar (table) provides an invitation to explore such questions in the context of the children's own church and the inner space of their own spiritual life today.

SPECIAL NOTES

This lesson sits on its own shelf, which is not as wide as the other shelves and is a bit taller. This is so children can stand and look into the church model through the front door or in through the windows at their eye level. The shelf is only a bit larger than the model. Below the top shelf, where the model of the church sits, are shelves that contain pictures of churches, books about stained glass, and other things of interest related to churches.

The model is heavy and the towers are likely to fall off when it is carried, so the children need help to get this lesson set up on the floor to work with on their own. This needs to be done on the floor or a large, low table, because, as the church is taken apart, space is needed for the removed pieces to be placed until they are used again when the church is rebuilt.

WHERE TO FIND THE MATERIALS

The shelf on which the model of the church sits is best placed near the Pentecost shelf and the shelf where the lessons about the saints are kept. This implies a fully developed Godly Play room. Creativity is needed to make adjustments when this is not the situation in your Godly Play program.

Sometimes "The Church" will be purchased by one's diocese or other judicatory and can be borrowed to give the lesson. Larger churches with developed programs may also share this lesson with smaller parishes. When such sharing takes place you might begin the lesson for the day with "The Church" already in the middle of the circle.

WHERE TO FIND MATERIALS

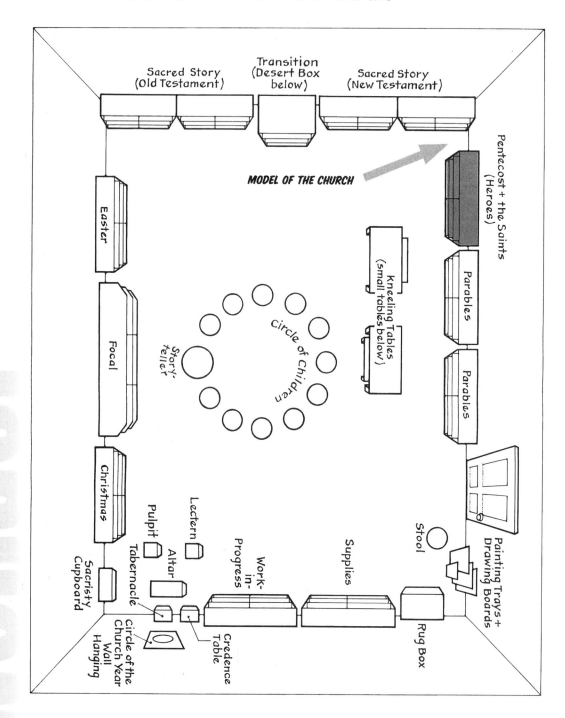

Sacred Story (Old Testament)

Transition (Desert Box below)

Sacred Story (New Testament)

MODEL OF THE CHURCH

Pentecost + the Saints (Heroes)

Easter

Parables

Parables

Story-teller

Circle of Children

kneeling Tables (small tables below)

Focal

Christmas

Sacristy Cupboard

Pulpit

Lectern

Altar

Tabernacle

Work-in-Progress

Supplies

Stool

Painting Trays + Drawing Boards

Circle of the Church Year Wall Hanging

Credence Table

Rug Box

MOVEMENTS

WORDS

Get a rug from the rug box to act as an ⟱ This lesson needs a rug.
underlay for the model of the church.
You may need a special rug if your nor-
mal ones are not large enough. Take
your time. Smooth it out. You then go
get the lesson.

Bring the model to the circle. Be careful. ⟱ Look. Here is the lesson. It is heavy. If you choose this for your work
It is heavy and the towers may fall off as you may need help. Watch out for the towers! They might fall off
you carry it. You will also need the basket when you are carrying it.
with parts of the model not yet in use.
Place the model on the underlay and the
basket beside you.

Place the model so the main doorway is
toward the children, so they can imagine
themselves going inside.

Sit back and look at the model. Let your
eyes run over all the details.

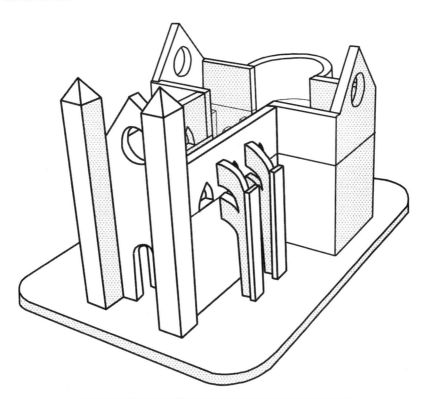

COMPLETELY ASSEMBLED MODEL OF THE CHURCH MATERIAL
(FROM THE CHILDREN'S PERSPECTIVE)

MOVEMENTS	WORDS
Pick up the altar (table). Look at it and then place it in various places with a smile, playfully trying out places where it might go.	This is a table for Holy Communion. It is sometimes called an *altar* and sometimes *a table*. I wonder where it goes? Where is it in our church?
Put the altar where it is located in your church.	
Pause a moment to show that you are about to begin the lesson. As you begin, you may want to acknowledge the shape of your own church if the children have not already done this.	There are many kinds of churches. Sometimes they look like this and sometimes they are different. When people see a church like *this*, they sometimes think that this is the way churches are supposed to look, but it is really just one shape in a long story of holy spaces.
Begin with the altar in the curved end.	
Remove the two towers. Lay them beside you on the floor.	Did you know there was a time when churches did not have towers?
Move your hand over where the roof would be.	The roof of a church like that was high and long.
Show where the windows are.	Here are the openings for the tall windows. See the big round windows at each end?
Remove the upper sections of the transepts and the apse.	When the church was built tall it had to have braces to hold up the high walls. Let's take all this away, too.
Reach into the basket and take out the long pieces of wood and slide them into the open spaces for the windows.	Now watch closely.
Remove from the basket the piece of wood with the rows of columns on it and place it in the nave. Put the two smaller sets of columns in the transepts.	
	Now we have a church with solid walls and tiny windows. This kind of church also was full of pillars to hold up the heavy stone roof.

MOVEMENTS ·   WORDS

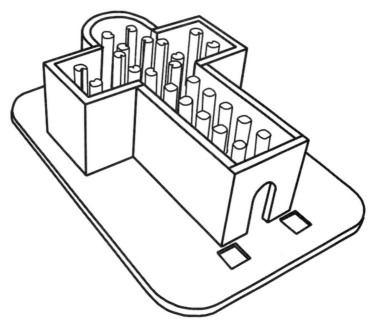

**MODEL OF THE CHURCH IN THE SHAPE OF A CROSS
(FROM THE CHILDREN'S PERSPECTIVE)**

Trace the cross shape of the space.

⟹ We still have the shape of a cross, but now when people look up from inside, the ceiling is flat. Can you imagine how that felt?

Remove the two transepts.

⟹ Churches were not always shaped like a cross. There was a time when they looked like this.

Slide the pieces of wood into the sides of the round church. This suggests that the walls of the basilica are extended in the model where you just removed the transepts. Motion to the places where the transepts were.

This kind of church was one long building, called a basilica. You have to pretend a little to see these openings as walls.

MOVEMENTS	WORDS

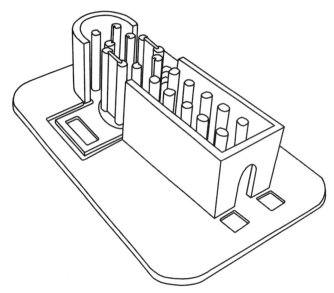

**MODEL OF THE CHURCH IN A LONG SHAPE
(FROM THE CHILDREN'S PERSPECTIVE)**

The bishop sat in his chair in the curved part to teach. This is also where the altar (table) was.

Remove the basilica's walls and curved end, leaving only the small round church. To complete the round church take out two more strips and place them in the remaining two slots to suggest that it has solid walls. Place the altar (table) in the center of it with the pulpit beside it. ➡ There was also a time when churches were not long. They were round.

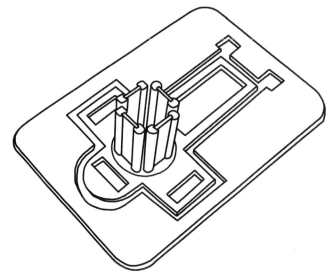

**MODEL OF THE CHURCH IN A ROUND SHAPE
(FROM THE STORYTELLER'S PERSPECTIVE)**

MOVEMENTS	WORDS
Remove the little round church. All that is left is the altar (table) standing alone on the empty base of the model.	I wonder what there was before the little round churches?

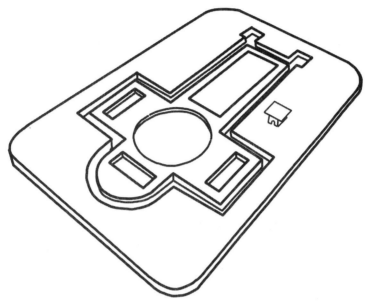

**MODEL OF THE CHURCH AS NO PHYSICAL SHAPE
(FROM THE STORYTELLER'S PERSPECTIVE)**

Take away the altar (table).	In the early days there were no special buildings. People gathered where they could. They met secretly in homes, on a hillside, in caves, or even underneath the ground in the catacombs of Rome.
Pause.	
Move your hand over the base to show the lack of any shape for the church at all.	
Place your hands, palms down, on the base with its empty places.	Before that there was nothing.

MOVEMENTS

WORDS

In 70 C.E. the Romans destroyed the Temple and the whole city of Jerusalem. It was awful. Most of the people who lived there were killed and the city was burned. You can still find broken stones and burned doorways in the city from those terrible days.

What were they going to do? There was no Temple, no priests, and no plan to guide their worship. There was only a scary silence and broken rocks.

The Temple and the Tabernacle before it were like boxes inside of boxes, as there is a parable inside a parable, inside a parable. What would the new shape be?

Replace the table on the base.

Both the Jews and the Jewish-Christians had worshiped in the Temple. Where could they go now? They began to meet in their homes, mostly in secret. The Romans were now after both the Jews and the Christians.
They were angry, because the Jews and the Jewish-Christian would not worship the Roman gods.

Place the table in various places around the base of the model.

The Jews kept the Passover in their homes and built synagogues. The Christians also gathered in their homes to share the holy bread and wine and to tell their stories.

The Roman Emperor Constantine finally made a law that it was okay to be a Christian, so Christians began to gather for worship without being afraid.

They read the stories of Jesus and the letters of Paul, as well as the Psalms and other things they knew so well from their Jewish days. They also gathered food and money to share with the poor. When it was time for people to be baptized they often went to rivers, as Jesus did when he was baptized by his cousin John.

Sometimes people left home to worship. They made pilgrimages to where holy things had happened or where holy people were buried, like people called martyrs, who were killed for being Christians.

Sometimes they built shrines, little churches, in those holy places, so people could gather around what was most important there.

MOVEMENTS   **WORDS**

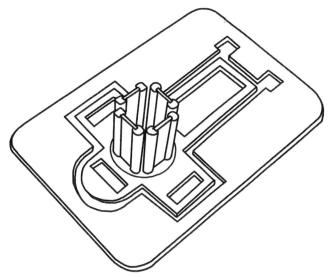

**MODEL OF THE CHURCH IN A ROUND SHAPE
(FROM THE STORYTELLER'S PERSPECTIVE)**

Replace the round church. Put the altar/ ➧ Sometimes a table for the bread and wine was put in the center.
table inside. Today some churches are still round. Perhaps, you have even been in
one.

Replace the walls of the basilica. Remove ➧ The Emperor Constantine gave the Christians some of the Roman
the wooden strips from the front and law buildings for their churches. They were called basilicas and
back of the round church, but leave the looked like this. The bishop sat in the curved end to teach and give
ones on the sides. Put in the columns. the people the holy bread and wine.
Point to where the bishop sat and place
the altar (table) in the curved part—the
apse.

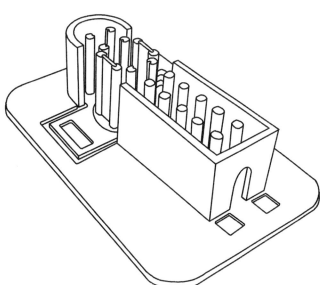

**MODEL OF THE CHURCH IN A LONG SHAPE
(FROM THE CHILDREN'S PERSPECTIVE)**

MOVEMENTS	WORDS
Point to the straight line of the church	This shape was straight like a road. People stood and sometimes sat in the church. When it was time for Holy Communion they made a little pilgrimage to the front in the same way as the people who made a big pilgrimage to Jerusalem.

By the time there were also priests. They read the scriptures. They preached and led the prayers. Money was collected for the poor and they gave the bread and wine to the people when the bishop was not there. Baptisms were now done mostly in or near the church. They used a big stone basin filled with water rather than a river or a pond. |
| *Replace the transepts to the basilica. Put in the additional columns.* | When Christians began to build their own churches they sometimes made them in the shape of a strong cross with thick walls and a solid roof, like a fortress. They wanted to feel safe inside. |
| *Point to the crossing.* | Today there are still churches in the shape of a cross, like a fortress. Maybe you have been in a church like that. The place where the long part and the short part meet is called *the crossing*. |

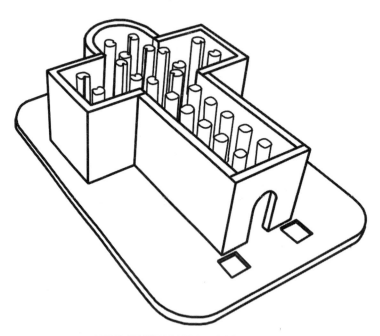

**MODEL OF THE CHURCH IN A CROSS SHAPE
(FROM THE CHILDREN'S PERSPECTIVE)**

People worshiped in these churches for hundreds of years, but then some wanted to show that God is as big as the sky, so they built the walls higher and higher.

MOVEMENTS	WORDS
Add the walls with the flying buttresses. Pull out the long wooden strips to make the windows. Replace all the Gothic pieces.	They made a lofty cross to be inside of, so the bigness of God could be inside of them. The walls had beautiful glass windows full of shapes, each one with a story.
Take away all the columns.	People still made their little pilgrimages to the altar, but after one thousand five hundred years in some churches, the elders began to bring the holy bread and holy wine to the people instead of having them go to the priests to receive these sacraments.

In the church in Geneva, where John Calvin was a leader, the table and the place for preaching were placed at the crossing, so people could gather around them. His chair was there, too, and it is still there today. |
| *Replace the towers.* | On the front of these high churches great towers were sometimes built to help people look upward when they went inside to pray and remember that God is larger than any building.

Sometimes people still build churches like this. Perhaps, you have been inside one of these, too. |

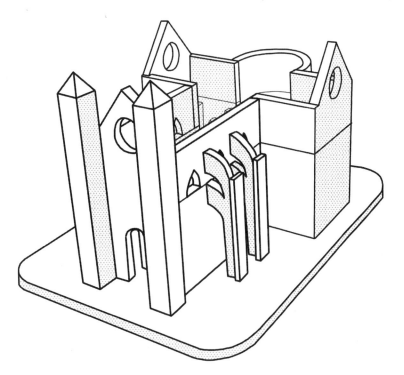

**COMPLETELY ASSEMBLED MODEL OF THE CHURCH MATERIAL
(FROM THE CHILDREN'S PERSPECTIVE)**

MOVEMENTS

WORDS

Sit back. Pause. Being the wondering.

➠ I wonder what part of this story you like best?

I wonder what part is the most important part?

I wonder where you are in the story? What part of the story is about how *you* feel in church?

I wonder if there is any part of the story we can leave out and still have all the story we need?

I wonder if you can find parts of this story in our own church?

I wonder what we *really* need to have, to have a church?

When the wondering is finished take the ➠ I wonder what you would like to make your work today?
church back to its place near the Pente-
cost shelf and invite the children to get
out their work.

LESSON 15

THE LITURGICAL SYNTHESIS

LESSON NOTES

FOCUS:
- **LITURGICAL ACTION**
- **SYNTHESIS LESSON**

THE MATERIAL
- **LOCATION: VARIOUS LOCATIONS THROUGHOUT THE CLASSROOM**
- **PIECES: "THE CIRCLE OF THE CHURCH YEAR" (WALL CALENDAR), "CIRCLE OF THE HOLY EUCHARIST," "HOLY BAPTISM," AND "THE HOLY FAMILY"**
- **UNDERLAY: "THE CIRCLE OF THE CHURCH YEAR" (WALL CALENDAR)**

BACKGROUND

This presentation superimposes a total of five "materials"—including the circle of children—so that children can synthesize the key presentations of the Liturgical Action materials in their mastery of the Christian language system. These five materials are all circles. They are the circle of the children, the church year, the Holy Eucharist, Baptism, and the Holy Family. This gives depth and liturgical orientation to the transformational core of the Christian language system. This lesson is for older children who are familiar with all the presentations on which this synthesis is based.

NOTES ON THE MATERIAL

The materials used in this presentation are located throughout the room and include the wall calendar for the "Circle of the Church Year" (Vol. 2, Lesson 1), the "Circle of the Holy Eucharist" (Vol. 4, Lesson 12), "Holy Baptism" (Vol. 3, Lesson 6), and "The Holy Family" (Vol. 2, p. 34). Each lesson is superimposed on the next in the middle of the circle of children. Unlike other lessons, you do not bring everything to the circle before beginning, but gather things as you need them. Note that ideally the green underlay used for the Circle of the Holy Eucharist lesson here is slightly smaller and fits within The Circle of the Church Year calendar as the lesson is presented.

SPECIAL NOTES

Before class you may need to be sure you can remove the wall calendar with ease. A second reminder is to be sure there is water in the pitcher that sits on the tray for Holy Baptism. Please also check to see if you have matches to light the candle.

This lesson is lengthy and is meant for experienced Godly Players. You will probably need to skip the work period and move directly to the feast after putting the materials away.

MOVEMENTS

Go and get the large "Circle of the Church Year Wall Calendar" and place it in the middle of the circle of children.

WORDS

Watch where I go to get the lesson for today. There are many parts to it, so be alert. This is a Synthesis lesson, so it will pull together many other lessons in the room, including you!

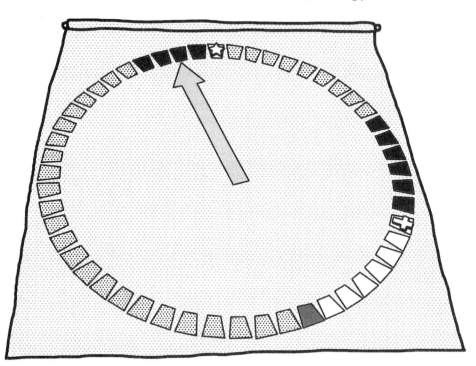

THE CIRCLE OF THE CHURCH YEAR (VIEW FROM THE CHILDREN'S PERSPECTIVE)

Motion with your hand to show the circle of children seated around the calendar, and then the wall hanging itself.

We now have two circles, don't we?
You make one and the lesson makes one.

MOVEMENTS	WORDS
	Now watch. There is more.
Go and get the "Circle of the Holy Eucharist." Spread out the green under-lay in the middle of the wall calendar. Place the plaque that names the lesson ("The Holy Eucharist") at the top (from the children's point of view) of the green underlay—the part closest to you.	Here is the "Circle of the Holy Eucharist."
Pick up the plaque that shows Jesus read-ing the scroll and hold it in your hands so the children can see it. Then place it in the middle of the green underlay.	This lesson begins with a story, doesn't it. Do you remember how Jesus came back from the desert and went to the synagogue in Nazareth? He unrolled the scroll of Isaiah and read the part about the coming of the Messiah. He told them it had happened! You know what happened next.
Pick up the plaque of the Last Supper and hold it in your hands just like the first one. Then place it in the middle of the green underlay above the plaque of Jesus reading the scroll.	Jesus then gathered The Twelve to help him and did many wonderful things, but then he had to go to Jerusalem for the last time.
	On Thursday evening during Holy Week, Jesus and the Twelve met in an upper room. After they had everything they wanted to eat and drink, Jesus showed them the holy bread and the holy wine. He said something like, "Whenever you share the bread and wine, I will be there."
	And so the Holy Eucharist has two parts.
Point to the orange card of the syna-gogue already placed at the center of the underlay.	First there is the Liturgy of the Word, when we read from the scriptures and hear the sermon.
Then place the plaque for "the Word of God" in the circle nearest to you at the top (from the point of view of the children).	
Point to the yellow card of the upper room already placed at the center of the underlay, then place the card for "Holy	Second, there is the Liturgy of Holy Communion.

MOVEMENTS

Communion" near the bottom of the circle (from the child's point of view).

Smoothly and quickly lay down all the cards, saying only a word or two to identify each part.

Smoothly and quickly lay down all the cards, saying only a word or two to identify each part.

The green underlay now has cards all around its circumference.

WORDS

Here is what happens during the Liturgy of the Word.

Here is what happens during the Liturgy of Holy Communion.

Now, I wonder how this circle fits into the larger circle of the church year? I wonder how we fit into both circles? I wonder what is in the Holy Eucharist that belongs in the Church Year and what is in the Church Year that belongs in the Holy Eucharist? I wonder where you fit into these two circles?

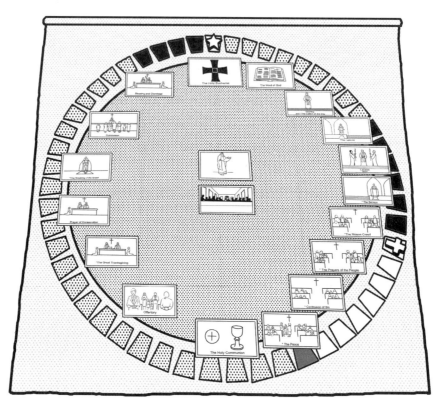

ADDING THE CIRCLE OF THE HOLY EUCHARIST (VIEW FROM THE CHILDREN'S PERSPECTIVE)

MOVEMENTS

WORDS

As the wondering begins to die down, pause and then sit back to signal more is coming.

Get the tray from the focal shelf containing the materials for Holy Baptism.

Lay out the three white circles in the center of the Circle of the Holy Eucharist. This covers the cards in the center of the presentation, so be careful when you place the materials on them. The surface is uneven.

Now watch…

Touch each of the three circles after naming them once and then point to each one as you name them again.

Inside the three circles we already have here we add three more circles.

Place the glass bowl on the Father circle, the Christ Candle on the Son circle, and the dove and oil on the Holy Spirit circle. Do this slowly and with deliberation.

Remember…we baptize people in the name of the Father, and the Son, and the Holy Spirit.

The Creator, the Redeemer, and the Sustainer.

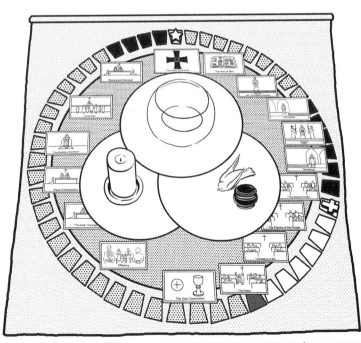

ADDING THE BAPTISM LESSON MATERIALS (VIEW FROM THE CHILDREN'S PERSPECTIVE)

MOVEMENTS

Pour the water into the glass bowl, listening to the sound of the water. Then put your hand in the water and move it as you begin to name it. Then cup your hand to draw out some water and pour it back as you continue.

When you have contemplated this for a moment, take a match from its container and point to the Christ Candle.

Strike the match and light the Christ candle.

Pick up the dove and "fly" it gently around the circle with your hand. Place it back on its own white circle and pick up the oil. Remove its stopper and then move the container slowly around the circle so children can "catch" its fragrance.

Sit back. Pause. Look around the room.

Get up and go all the way around the room. Touch or pick up various materials and replace them, shaking your head "No." You finally arrive back at the altar/focal shelf. You touch the Holy Family.

Sit back down in the circle and reach behind you to pick the figures of the Holy Family and the figure of the Risen Christ as you name them and wonder at their significance. Place the group in the center of the three overlapping circles as you name them.

Pick up the Christ Child and the manger. Hold them in the palm of your hand for all the children to see.

WORDS

This is the water of creation, and the dangerous water of the flood. This is the water the people went through into freedom. This is the water Jesus was baptized in. It is also the water you were—or will be—baptized in, and there is so much more.

There was once someone who said such amazing things and did such wonderful things that people just had to ask him who he was. One time when they asked him who he was, he said...

"...I am the Light."

The Holy Spirit goes where it will. It rides the wind like a dove and is invisible, like the scent of this oil, but it is always there.

This is a lot, but I wonder if there is more?

Now watch.

Here is the Holy Family.

This is the Christ Child. He is holding out his arms to give you a hug.

MOVEMENTS	WORDS
Place the Christ Child and the manger in the middle of the circle where the three circles from Baptism overlap. As you bring the other figures down, place them in a circle around the Christ child.	
Next, hold Mary in the palm of your hand and show her to the children and then place her.	Here is the Mother Mary.
Hold Joseph in the palm of your hand and show him to the children and then place him.	Here is the Father Joseph.
Hold out the donkey and place it.	Here is the donkey that Mary rode when she and Joseph went to Bethlehem.
Hold out the cow and then place it with the other figures around of the manger.	Here is the cow that was in the stable when the baby was born.
Hold out the shepherd and the sheep and then place them around the manger.	Here is a shepherd who saw the great light and heard the angels sing. There were more shepherds than this, but we will put down one to remind us. Here are some sheep. There were many more, but these will help us remember.
Pick up each of the three kings and show them to the children. Then place them with the other figures.	Here are the three kings, the wise men. They brought gifts for the Christ Child: gold, frankincense, and myrrh.
Pick up the figure of the Risen Christ from the focal shelf and place it behind the Holy Family (from the children's perspective). You then superimpose the baby with outstretched arms on the risen Christ with outstretched arms.	Here is the little baby reaching out to give you a hug. He grew up to be a man and died on the cross for us. That is very sad, but is also wonderful, in an Easter kind of way.
Place the Christ Child back in the manger.	Now he can reach out and give the whole world a hug. Not just back then and there, but now and everywhere.

MOVEMENTS   **WORDS**

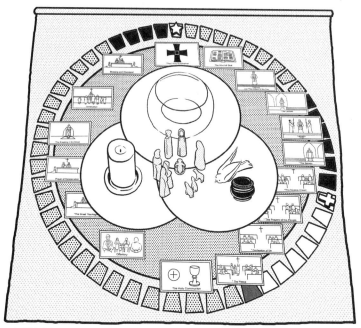

**WITH THE CIRCLE OF THE HOLY FAMILY, BEFORE ADDING THE RISEN CHRIST
(VIEW FROM THE CHILDREN'S PERSPECTIVE)**

Pause.

Sit back and contemplate the whole les- ➡ I wonder what part of this lesson you like the best?
son. Then begin to wonder.

I wonder what part is most important?

I wonder what part is about you, or what part you are in?

I wonder if we could leave any part out and still have all that we need?

I wonder where you are in all these circles? Where is our circle?

I wonder which circle you like best?

I wonder which circle is about you?

I wonder where you are in all these circles?

I wonder what would happen if we left out any of the circles?

I wonder if you have even seen anything from any of these circles in the church?

MOVEMENTS

When the wondering dies down, sit back and begin to look around the room.

Replace the parts of the lesson on the shelves, moving in reverse order.

When everything is put away check the time and if there is time for a work period you can invite the children to get out their work.

WORDS

Now it is time to put everything back. This will take a long time. Let's just enjoy watching what happens. Are you ready? Okay, let's begin.

I wonder what you would like to make your work today?

APPENDIX

This Appendix is divided into two parts. The first section summarizes the foundational literature and the second outlines the spiral curriculum as it is known currently. These two overviews bring the development of Godly Play up to date as the ten-year publishing project of the eight volumes of *The Complete Guide To Godly Play* comes to a close.

SECTION 1. GODLY PLAY: THE FOUNDATIONAL LITERATURE

This summary of Godly Play's foundational literature is organized around the following topics: the key assumption, an introduction, three overlapping historical contexts, the Biblical theology, the method, the theory conceived of as spiritual guidance, and the exploration of children's spirituality.

THE KEY ASSUMPTION

Hans Urs von Balthasar, *Unless You Become Like This Child* (1991)
David Hay, *Something There: The Biology of the Human Spirit* (2007)
Edward Robinson, *The Original Vision: A Study of the Religious Experience of Childhood* (1983)

The key assumption of Godly Play is that young children already have experienced the presence of the mystery of God when their spiritual guidance (or lack of it) begins at an early age. This experience is undifferentiated. Children need to learn an appropriate language for identifying this experience, expressing it, naming it, and evaluating it by becoming part of a community of support and mentoring to develop the art of how to use this language to guide themselves in community toward spiritual maturity.

Godly Play is, therefore, truly *spiritual guidance*. The adult walks alongside the child on the journey of life, a more experienced guide to be sure, but one who is also still growing and seeking God's elusive presence. The child and the adult move forward with mutual blessing toward the "Kingdom" Jesus spoke of. The adult cannot make this journey for the child, but can only equip the child for the time when the adult can no longer be available as a mentor. The primary kind of "equipment" needed is Christian language that still flows from Jesus' life, history, and way of speaking.

Since Godly Play is spiritual guidance it does not attempt to force, manipulate, convince, or bribe children to think and feel that God is present in their lives. God's living reality is already part of their experience, so what children need is an invitation into a supportive environment to learn the art of making God's presence more conscious and available. The goal is not to teach "Christianity" but to teach the art of how to use Christianity's kind of communication to cope with one's existential limits such as death, aloneness, the threat of freedom, and the need for an existentially meaningful way to live. To teach this language as an end in itself would be idolatry. That is not what Godly Play intends.

Godly Play is a spiritual practice. It encourages the mutual blessing of children and adults because, as Jesus said, children show the way into the reality he called "the Kingdom" and when we welcome them we welcome him and the one who sent him. This is why being close to children helps both youth and adults to be more mature spiritually. When youth and adults are more mature spiritually they are better able to help children flourish. When children flourish spiritually, this in turn helps adults mature spiritually. The mutual blessing expands and deepens. Youth and adults who do not have children in their community, therefore, need to seek them out as a spiritual practice.

The *theological* appreciation of children's experiences of God has been sparse in the history of the church, but the Swiss, Roman Catholic theologian Hans Urs von Balthasar urged, during the twentieth century, that children first know God in their mother's smile. His *Unless You Become Like This Child* was the last of his many great books and is a concentrated statement about how children and Jesus as a child are important for the lives of all Christians.

Evidence has also been accumulating in the *physical and social sciences* that the evolution of our species has been able to continue, because we are fundamentally spiritual beings. David Hay's book articulates this position and connects it with the work of Alister Hardy, the late Oxford zoologist and founder of the Religious Experience Research Unit at Oxford. RERU is now called the "Alister Hardy Religious Experience Research Centre" after its founder and it is located at the University of Wales, Trinity Saint David.

David Hay's book *Something There: The Biology of the Human Spirit* and his biography of Alister Hardy, *God's Biologist,* provide a serious challenge to the irrational prejudice against acknowledging the presence of the mystery of God in our lives. This prejudice developed especially during the eighteenth century in the Western intellectual tradition. When people look beyond this taboo the question is no longer whether God is present, but becomes how to introduce the language of religion to children in a constructive way. This needs to be done in a way that does not stunt, distort, inhibit, or even destroy children's ability to add religious richness and maturity to our species. Godly Play is a way to do that for Christians and its method might be fruitfully adapted for any of the other major religions on this earth. Godly Play invites children into a kind of playful orthodoxy that combines a deep rooting in well-tested, classical Christian language with an openness to and interest in new people, new ideas, new ways of thinking, and the future. This is accomplished by associating the art of using Christian language with the creative process to make existential meaning while it is being learned.

Edward Robinson's book *The Original Vision* preceded Hay's, just as Robinson preceded him as director of The Religious Experience Research Unit in Oxford. Robinson stayed close to the reports of children's experiences of God on which his view of "the original vision" is based and they support his argument that God is present in the child's original vision of reality.

The centering of Godly Play around the experience of God is conceived of in a classical way. It appreciates that God—who is beyond, beside, and within—is the central, empirical reference for Christian language, which provides the best way to discover and develop God's presence in ones life. All three ways of knowing God are present and acknowledged in Godly Play all the time, although one kind of awareness usually dominates the other two at different times in one's life and even during the hours of a single day. Godly Play is, therefore, deeply Trinity-centered in its basic assumption.

AN INTRODUCTION TO GODLY PLAY

Jerome W. Berryman, *Godly Play: An Imaginative Approach to Religious Education* (1995)

This book introduces the reader to the theory and practice of Godly Play. It combines developmental psychology and Montessori education with God's lively presence, theology, play, and the creative process to articulate an approach for mentoring children to become maturing Christians.

Godly Play discusses "the ultimate game," the importance of laughter, and the structure of a Godly Play experience. It also discusses six aspects of the spoken and unspoken "lessons" in terms of wonder, community/ethics, the participants' existential limits, the nature of religious language, the importance of associating religious language with the creative process for the making of existential meaning, and the Holy Eucharist as the deep structure for the Godly Play approach to the spiritual guidance of children (and adults).

This introduction is really two books in one. There is the primary text for everyone, but there are also extensive footnotes in the back of the book for the scholar.

THE HISTORICAL CONTEXTS FOR GODLY PLAY

Jerome W. Berryman, *Children and the Theologians* (2009)
Jerome W. Berryman, *The Spiritual Guidance of Children: Montessori, Godly Play and the Future* (2013)
E. M. Standing, *The Child in the Church* (1965)
Brendan Hyde, *The Search for a Theology of Childhood: Essays by Jerome Berryman from 1978-2009.* (in press, 2012)

The historical context for Godly Play has three levels. *Children and the Theologians* provides the big picture, by examining selected theologians' views of children from the church's history. The themes of a *de facto* doctrine of children emerge from this study. They are *ambivalence, ambiguity, indifference,* and *grace.* This *implied* doctrine still influences us today, so its force needs to be acknowledged in a conscious way and an *explicit* alternative needs to be articulated. This book calls for children to be understood as a means of grace. They provide ways for mutual blessing between the generations to help reveal Jesus (and the one who sent him) as well as "the Kingdom" Jesus spoke of. This revelation is communicated by how children are, as much as by what they say and do.

The second level of the historical context for Godly Play is the history of Maria Montessori's interest in children's religious education. It is important to see how Godly Play fits into the four generations of the development of Montessori's ideas, materials, and practice in this area. A concise collection of primary sources for understanding this history may be found in E. M. Standing's *The Child in the Church*, which includes chapters by Maria Montessori, Standing, Sofia Cavalletti, and others.

The third level of historical context is the specific development of Godly Play. Brendan Hyde's book *The Search for a Theology of Childhood: Essays by Jerome W. Berryman from 1978-2009* traces the growth of Godly Play through a series of previously published articles.

THE BIBLICAL THEOLOGY

Samuel Terrien, *The Elusive Presence: Toward a New Biblical Theology* (1978)

There are many approaches to Biblical theology. The one selected for Godly Play is that of Samuel Terrien, because of his emphasis on the experience of God over thousands of years rather than the theology that developed from that experience. This is more organically related to what the child is experiencing and provides a meaningful story that is like the child's own story. Terrien wrote, "When presence is 'guaranteed' to human senses or reason, it is no longer real presence. The proprietary sight of the glory destroys the vision, whether in the temple of Zion or in the eucharistic body. … In biblical faith, presence eludes but does not delude" (476).

Children know this elusive presence, but they have few opportunities to learn an adequate language to identify, name, express or gain perspective on it. Most of the language they learn in school is the language of science, including the social sciences, and outside of school they are taught the language of consumers. Classical Christian language, including the Hebrew Bible, is made available to them by Godly Play in a way that allows them to discover, name, discuss, and evaluate these experiences as connected to their own experience of God's elusive presence. Organizing Godly Play's curriculum around the child's journey and the Biblical journey gives children a sense that what they have experienced spiritually has a vast and rich connection with the larger narrative of the Bible and the church.

THE METHOD

Jerome W. Berryman, *Teaching Godly Play: How to Mentor the Spiritual Development of Children* (2009)

This book is the expanded and rewritten second edition of a 1995 publication. It is the most complete statement of the Godly Play method and, like the first edition, it is organized around what actually happens in a Godly Play room. It combines this process with background information about why adult mentors need to make certain moves when guiding children's spirituality. It also includes ways of evaluating ones practice of spiritual guidance and how to keep growing as a mentor.

THE THEORY

Jerome W. Berryman, *Playful Orthodoxy: A Theory for the Spiritual Guidance of Children (manuscript in preparation)*

Religious education is reframed in this manuscript as spiritual guidance. Four principles are examined as aids for such guidance: authentic presence, wise communication, mutual blessing, and ethical speaking/being. These four principles are integrated through deep play with God and the attachment of classical Christian language to the creative process, which is our fundamental identity, as creatures fashioned in the Creator's image. The goal of such mentoring is the graceful person.

This approach to spiritual guidance helps children become deeply grounded in classical Christian language *and at the same time* enables and supports their wonder about God's presence, and openness to new people, to new ideas and to the future while they are learning this language. The integration of experience and language involved in Godly Play helps children begin to live and think as Christians in a playfully orthodox way. The goal for children involved in this kind of spiritual guidance is to enter adolescence with an inner working model of the Christian language system that both deeply grounds them and yet leaves them open and stimulates them for continued growth all their life long so that they can be graceful people.

CHILDREN'S SPIRITUALITY

Rebecca Nye, *Children's Spirituality: What It Is and Why It Matters* (2009)
Jerome W. Berryman, *A General Theory of Children's Spirituality (manuscript in preparation)*

Rebecca Nye's book is well grounded in the questions that people ask about children's spirituality. It is wise not only in this sense but also in its seasoned ability to connect the lives of children with adult spirituality. Dr. Nye is a child psychologist, as well as a Godly Play trainer, and her book looks at children's spirituality from a psychological as well as a spiritual point of view in a way that is both helpful and inspiring.

A General Theory of Children's Spirituality is a complement to Dr. Nye's book. It brings together the perspectives on children's spirituality of theologians, historians, psychologists, educators, and of autobiography, including the remembered experience one's own childhood.

Two additional manuscripts in preparation for publication amplify the autobiographical perspective of this general theory. One is by John Pridmore concerning children's spirituality in autobiography and the other is by Robert Hurley concerning children's spirituality in books written for children. This literary approach to understanding children's spirituality is often overlooked by more science-oriented methods for understanding the same phenomenon. The sensitivity of poets and novelists, as well as their gift of language, enables nuances in children's spirituality to be discovered that objectivity and mathematics may miss.

CONCLUDING REMARKS ABOUT THE FOUNDATIONAL LITERATURE

There is a growing body of critique concerning Godly Play's foundations, which is welcome and important. The minimum basis for such critiques should include, at least, a response to this summary of the foundational literature and how it is put into action in the actual practice of Godly Play. This practice is *introduced* in the core trainings provided by the Godly Play Foundation, but *experienced* with children. With this in mind we turn now to an overview of the Godly Play curriculum.

SECTION 2. GODLY PLAY: THE SPIRAL CURRICULUM

The following outline of the curriculum is organized in two ways. First, the Core, the Extensions, Enrichments, and Synthesis lessons are laid out horizontally, in parallel columns. The parallel columns are also grouped vertically according to the four genres, as well as the lessons after the Biblical era, and lessons for the home and other settings. A discussion about each kind of lesson concludes this overview.

This full outline of the spiral curriculum marks the end of a ten-year publishing project begun in 2002 with *Volume 1* of *The Complete Guide To Godly Play*. It is the most complete statement of an overview to date, but the development of the curriculum continues.

CORE PRESENTATIONS	EXTENSIONS	ENRICHMENTS	SYNTHESIS
(3-6, 6-9, 9-12 years)	(6-9, 9-12 years)	(6-9, 9-12 years)	(9-12 years)

SACRED STORIES

A Sacred Story is one in which God is a character. We tell the stories of how the people met God in creation, with the patriarchs, in the Exodus, at Sinai, in the Temple, in the prophets' visions, in The Word, and elsewhere.

The Holy Family—This presentation sits on the focal/altar shelf in the center on the top shelf. It includes dimensions of all four genres, since it is a story, a liturgical experience, is parabolic, and invites contemplative silence. This is the axis of the Christian language system, which shows, by its concise integration of the birth, death, and resurrection of our Lord, the way open to the future. An extension for the Holy Family is Mary, The Mother of Jesus.

The Circle of the Church Year (mounted on the wall)			
The Circle of the Church Year (wooden material)	The Circle of the Church Year – Advanced	Books of the Bible (relates to the lectionary; shows how the Bible was "built" like shelves of books in a library)	*Sacred Story Synthesis*
The Creation	Second Creation: The Falling Apart		
The Great Family	Abraham Sarah Jacob Joseph		

CORE PRESENTATIONS	EXTENSIONS	ENRICHMENTS	SYNTHESIS
(3-6, 6-9, 9-12 years)	(6-9, 9-12 years)	(6-9, 9-12 years)	(9-12 years)

SACRED STORIES *(continued)*

A Sacred Story is one in which God is a character. We tell the stories of how the people met God in creation, with the patriarchs, in the Exodus, at Sinai, in the Temple, in the prophets' visions, in The Word, and elsewhere.

The Exodus	Moses		
The Ten Best Ways	Moses		
The Ark and the Tent	Ruth Samuel		
The Temple	David		
The Exile and Return			
The Prophets	Elijah Isaiah Jeremiah		
Wisdom/Apocalypse (in development)	Job Daniel		*Sacred Story* *Synthesis*
Psalms (in development)	David		

The Greatest Parable	Miracles
	   (in development)
	Beatitudes
	   (in development)		

Paul's Discovery			
Peter's Vision (in development)			

CORE PRESENTATIONS	EXTENSIONS	ENRICHMENTS	SYNTHESIS
(3-6, 6-9, 9-12 years)	(6-9, 9-12 years)	(6-9, 9-12 years)	(9-12 years)

LITURGICAL ACTION

Liturgy means literally, "the work of the people." Liturgy helps express inner and outer existential realities in a way that others can participate in. The Godly play approach includes lessons about Baptism and Holy Eucharist, as well as lessons about the liturgical seasons (Advent, Lent, Easter and Pentecost).

Advent I-V Epiphany	Mary	Mystery of Christmas	
Holy Baptism			
Faces of Easter	The Twelve	Mystery of Easter Jesus and Jerusalem Easter Eggs (developed after Biblical times)	Liturgical Action Synthesis
Knowing Jesus in a New Way	Pentecost		
The Good Shepherd & World Communion			
The Synagogue and the Upper Room			
The Circle of the Holy Eucharist	Symbols of the Holy Eucharist		

CORE PRESENTATIONS	EXTENSIONS	ENRICHMENTS	SYNTHESIS
(3-6, 6-9, 9-12 years)	(6-9, 9-12 years)	(6-9, 9-12 years)	(9-12 years)

PARABLES

A parable is a kind of riddle that uses short fiction to reference a transcendent symbol, which in the Gospels is generally the Kingdom of Heaven or Jesus. The Godly Play approach to parables includes six guiding parables in gold boxes, parables about parables, side-by-sides, the parable cards, and the parable games (which include all the Parables of Jesus and his "I am" statements).

Parable of the Good Shepherd The Parable of the Great Pearl Parable of the Sower The Parable of the Leaven The Parable of the Mustard Seed The Parable of the Good 　Samaritan	Parable of Parables The Deep Well Jesus' Sayings 　(in development) Parable Games	Side-by-Sides	*Parable Synthesis*

CONTEMPLATIVE SILENCE

This genre of classical Christian language is found in the way the lessons are presented. The mindfulness, measured pace, and leaving pauses contribute to this. The prayers and reflection during the feast are also examples.

The children are the "silence materials." The materials in the room must be silent. The children are the only ones in the room *who can choose* to be silent. Finally, there is a step in the presentation of "The Greatest Parable" that is explicitly silent.	*Contemplative Silence Synthesis**

*The synthesis lesson for contemplative silence is when the older children (9-12) are invited to go into the church to sit in silence scattered around the nave to see if they can be more aware of God's presence. They are asked to be alert to knowing God as the Holy Trinity—beyond them in their awareness of the creation, beside them in the Gospels as Jesus' presence with them as a redemptive companion, and within them as the Holy Spirit.

When the children are gathered for the wondering following this experience, the wondering is guided as follows: I wonder what part of this you liked best? I wonder what part was the most important? I wonder how much of you was really involved? I wonder what in the church helped or got in the way? I wonder whether you felt God's presence more beyond, as the Creator of the world, or more beside you as Jesus, or more as a power within as the Holy Spirit? I wonder how talking about this is different from the silence you experienced in the church?

CORE PRESENTATIONS	EXTENSIONS	ENRICHMENTS	SYNTHESIS
(3-6, 6-9, 9-12 years)	(6-9, 9-12 years)	(6-9, 9-12 years)	(9-12 years)

AFTER THE BIBLICAL ERA

These are sometimes called the "afterwards" lessons. They are about things and events that took place after the Biblical era.

The Part That Hasn't Been Written Yet

The Crosses

The Church

The Communion of Saints: This collection of saints is organized around a saint for each month, so the children can find their own birthdays alongside these saints. There are six men and six women. Many different personality types are also represented The representative masters of the spiritual life are as follows:

Afterwards Synthesis*

Thomas Aquinas	Augustine of Hippo
Valentine	Mother Teresa of Calcutta
St. Patrick	Teresa of Avila
Catherine of Siena	Margaret of Scotland
Julian of Norwich	Nicholas, bishop of Myra
Columba	The Story of the Child's Own Saint
Elizabeth of Portugal	The Story of the Child's Own Life

*The Afterwards Synthesis is for older children, 9-12 years. They are taken into the church and are invited to walk around in the church as a group with the co-teachers. At each significant part of the interior architecture the group stops and the storyteller invites wondering about where each part comes from. The stories in the windows are discussed. The altar/table placement is discussed. The crossing is discussed. What is behind and above the altar/table is discussed. The use of symbols is discussed. Each point of interest is touched, and talked about. The group then goes outside the church to look at the exterior architectural shape of the church and what it says to them and to the community around it.

SPECIAL PRESENTATION FOR THE GODLY PLAY CLASSROOM

The Right Rite: Choosing the Appropriate Liturgical Action for Life's Experience

SPECIAL PRESENTATIONS FOR THE HOME AND OTHER SETTINGS

These materials and presentations are designed especially for the home, mostly to be done around the table, like the Jewish Seder. They are also useful in additional settings, such as presenting the creation story on camping trips and other family outings.

These lessons resemble lessons found in a Godly Play room, but they are smaller and the presentations are much shorter. This is so the lesson can be laid out on a table when the "family" (however one may define that) is gathered for a meal. The lessons draw the family story into the Biblical Story. Adults or older children lead these small liturgies, which are accessible to all ages with a minimum amount of preparation by the leaders.

Advent: Preparing for the Mystery of Christmas

Lent: Preparing for the Mystery of Easter

Eastertide: Preparing for the Mystery of Pentecost (in development)

Creation

The Parable of the Good Shepherd

DEFINING THE KINDS OF LESSONS
IN THE GODLY PLAY CURRICULUM

I. DEFINITIONS:

"Core lessons" are the key sacred story, liturgical action, parable, and silence lessons. An example from the sacred story genre is "Creation."

The sacred stories follow the key events noted by Samuel Terrien's *The Elusive Presence*, which provides the Biblical theology for Godly Play. The liturgical action presentations generally follow the liturgical year. The parables follow the loosely organized collections in the Synoptic Gospels. The contemplative silence genre may be found in the way the lessons are presented, the organization of the room, and the whole process of Godly Play. The children and their mentors are the main embodiment of this genre.

"Extensions" extend the core lessons. They expand not only sacred stories but also the liturgical and parable lessons. An example is the story of "Ruth," which helps extend the narratives of "The Ark and the Tent" and "The Temple" toward each other by implicitly connecting them. All three extensions sit on the shelves below these lessons, since core lessons are displayed on the top shelf in the Godly Play room.

The materials for this type of lesson are all placed on strips, as they are told, because they can be laid alongside the core presentation, literally extending out from the core along the line of the story. The strips can all be joined together to connect with the core lessons to make a long timeline of the Biblical narrative. This is an impressive lesson, because it is too long to fit in most Godly Play rooms. It will have to be put together in the hallway or a larger room by a group of interested children.

"Enrichment" lessons do not extend so much as enrich or deepen the core lessons. This kind of lesson goes over the same material in a core lesson but from a different angle or in more detailed way. An example is using the model of Jerusalem to retell what was said about Holy Week during the presentation of "The Faces of Easter." This adds detail and locates the story more securely in its geographical setting of valleys and hills.

"Afterwards" lessons involve events and symbols that are not part of the Biblical era. An example is the variety of crosses that have been developed since the original Roman cross Jesus died on. Another example is the lesson about "The Church."

"Synthesis" lessons make a synthesis of key lessons in the four genres. The synthesis for the *sacred stories* integrates key narratives to make a lesson about the Holy Trinity. The synthesis lesson for the *parables* synthesizes all of the parables from the Synoptic Gospels and the "I am" statements from the Gospel of John around a series of questions concerning the whole corpus of parables and what they create as a whole. The synthesis for the *liturgical action* lessons draws together key liturgical lessons into a series of circles. The synthesis lesson for the *contemplative silence* genre takes the older children into the church to sit in silence and to see if they become more aware of God's presence and then to wonder together about what happened.

The *afterwards* lessons are slightly different, since they don't represent a particular genre of Biblical communication. These lessons build on the four genres of the foundational Christian communication system, but they evoke how this foundation has worked itself out in the history of the church. The synthesis lesson for this kind of communication, then, is to take the older children on tours of the church's interior and exterior to see how what is inside and outside draws on and evokes both the primary, Biblical communication and what has developed since then. An example is the shape of the church itself and what it communicates in its particular features and generally as a whole.

2. DISCUSSION OF THE DEFINITIONS:

There are, of course, overlaps in the definitions above. "Knowing Jesus in a New Way" is a good example. It is a core, liturgical action lesson, because it follows the liturgical structure of Eastertide and parallels the way the lessons for "The Faces" prepare for Easter during Lent. It continues "The Faces" by marking the next six Sundays in Eastertide to prepare the child for Pentecost. This is not merely a story about Jesus in the first century. It brings the experience of Pentecost into the present liturgically, rather than being relegated to past history. The artwork is different from "The Faces," because Jesus' presence is *suggested* by the faces of the disciples rather than by imagining Jesus' face during his life, death, and resurrection. The disciples slowly begin to understand what the empty tomb means, and they are in the same position relative to Jesus as we are, as we move from being sheep to shepherds.

Another overlap might be seen in "The Mystery of Pentecost." It is an extension of "Knowing Jesus in a New Way," because it extends Eastertide and Pentecost by adding the Tower of Babel to the narrative. The loss of a common language and God's presence extends "The Mystery of Pentecost" by sharpening the awareness of the unity that Jesus' presence gives those who communicate as Christians with the common language that flows from his life. This theme of our common language is also part of the background for "The Greatest Parable."

"The Greatest Parable" is a sacred story about the public ministry of Jesus, but it might also be thought of as an extension of "The Faces of Easter." It extends this core lesson, but it is more importantly the culmination of the sacred story about God's elusive presence that began with "Creation," so it is listed as a core lesson. "The Greatest Parable" not only tells the story of Jesus' public ministry but also acknowledges that the whole Christian language system flows out of Jesus' life, death, and resurrection, as well as his coming again. This lesson, then, has the whole Godly Play room as its extension *and* enrichment! This is why it is the most curious box in the whole room!

Another overlap can be illustrated by "Jesus and Jerusalem," thought of as an enrichment lesson. A schematic model of Jerusalem is used to trace Jesus' movements during Holy Week. It could be considered an extension of "The Faces," because it adds a few details to Jesus' journey during Holy Week. The model and map, however, do not add *substantially* to "The Faces." Instead, it provides a sensorial telling of what happened, using much the same language as used in "The Faces," so it is more an enrichment than an extension lesson.

These somewhat confusing overlaps are also a sign of the integration of the spiral curriculum. Overlapping themes, phrases, images, and other matters help draw together the Christian language system into a meaningful and appropriate set of tools for children's spiritual guidance.